EVERYDAY MEDIATOR

EVERYDAY MEDIATOR

SEVEN PRACTICES *for* NAVIGATING CONFLICT

Daniel Griffith

Everyday Mediator: Seven Practices for Navigating Conflict

Copyright ©2025 Daniel Griffith

All rights reserved. No portion of this book may be reproduced in any form, by any means, electronic or mechanical, including photocopying, recording, or by any information storage and retrieval system, without permission in writing from the publisher.

987654321
First Edition
Printed in the United States of America.

Cover design by Jake Clark, Pithy Wordsmithery
Interior layout by Joanna Beyer, Pithy Wordsmithery
Copyediting by Nils Kuehn, Pithy Wordsmithery
Proofreading by Scott Morrow, Pithy Wordsmithery

ISBN: 979-8-9995744-0-4 (paperback)
ISBN: 979-8-9995744-2-8 (e-book)
ISBN: 979-8-9995744-1-1 (hardcover)

Daniel Griffith
daniel@everydaymediator.com
Website: www.everydaymediator.com

Library of Congress Control Number: 2025915583

To Michelle,
Who shared the bumpy ride with me one day,

and

To Mary,
Who shares the bumpy ride with me every day.

"In *Everyday Mediator*, Daniel Griffith presents a practical road map for how we can help people address conflicts that occur in our day-to-day lives. He recognizes that all of us have the potential to be mediators in practice (if not in name) and provides useful tools and examples for how we can embrace that potential and thereby contribute to a better, more collaborative, and more peaceful world."

Bernie Mayer
    Author of *Staying with Conflict* and (with Jackie Font-Guzmán) *The Neutrality Trap*
    Founding Partner, CDR Associates, and Professor Emeritus of Conflict Studies, Creighton University

"In a world where friction and frustration can be part of so many relationships at work and at home, anything that creates better and more meaningful human connection is a plus. In *Everyday Mediator*, Dan brings to life the opportunities each of us have to help create more connection instead of division and harmony instead of conflict. Dan is an expert on mediation, and this book brings out his best ideas and recommendations for the benefit of us all."

Ben Eubanks
    Chief Research Officer, Lighthouse Research & Advisory
    2x Best-Selling Author of *The Payroll Promise* and *Talent Scarcity*
    Host of *We're Only Human Podcast*

"In many major cities, reports of fatal shootings are so often preceded by 'the two were arguing…' How much better if these sad scenarios, and so many other familiar conflicts, were instead resolved by peaceable conversation. Dan Griffith offers a down-to-earth, 'everyman' approach to mediation and conflict resolution. His message so richly deserves our attention and our engagement."

Haavi Morreim, JD, PhD
    Principal, Center for Conflict Resolution in Healthcare LLC
    TN Supreme Court Rule 31–Listed Mediator, Civil and Family

"Having benefited from Dan's mediation training, this book is a master class to help all people adapt these skills to everyday conversations. When conversations get uncomfortable is where growth begins. We need these tools to help us all get to the heart of what matters."

Kori Reed
    Director of Communication
    Award-Winning Author of *Men-in-the-Middle: Conversations to Gain Momentum with Gender Equity's Silent Majority*

"Too often, we rely on formal systems to navigate conflict—an approach that can be time-consuming and ultimately unsatisfying. *Everyday Mediator* offers a compelling alternative: informal, effective mediation led by everyday people motivated to help others reach mutually acceptable agreements."

Allison M. Vaillancourt, PhD
    Organizational Strategy Consultant and Author

"*Everyday Mediator* is an essential guide for anyone looking to make a tangible difference in their everyday interactions. It's not just a manual; it is an inspirational call to action. Griffith's passion for mediation shines through every page, encouraging readers to embrace their role as everyday mediators and make a meaningful impact in their communities. His approach is grounded in compassion, authenticity, and a deep belief in the transformative power of mediation. Whether you are a friend, colleague, or seasoned professional, this book will inspire you to step into the fray and help others find common ground."

Sissy Meredith, PhD
    Learning and Development Executive

"*Everyday Mediator* is written less for professional mediators and more for the rest of us, the everyday people who care deeply but do not always know how to help. Dan reminds us that we already have what it takes. The instincts, the presence, the ability to listen and to guide with authenticity and curiosity. He shows how these skills can be developed by every one of us and how to apply those skills in everyday life. We do not need more division. We need more people willing to be the steady third voice in the room. Dan hands us the cape."

Matthew Carroll
    President, Indiana Association of Mediators
    Mediation Faculty Member, Northwestern University and
        Aurora University
    Divorce and Civil Mediator

"Daniel Griffith delivers a timely and practical guide for anyone seeking to approach conflict with more compassion, clarity, and confidence. He invites us to see mediation not as a niche skill reserved for professionals or those with specific titles but as an everyday skill we can all practice. His writing is thoughtful, grounded, and accessible, offering practical tools and inspiration on how to approach the occasional messiness of real-world relationships, whether personal or professional. For anyone trying to bring more peace and understanding into the world, this book is well worth the read."

Kelly A. Cherwin
Director of Editorial Strategy, HigherEdJobs

"Dan Griffith is a great voice to share ideas on how best to work through challenging situations. He has been a great professional in the higher-education setting to bring people, policy, and practice together to build a respectful community. *Everyday Mediator* will provide Dan's common sense and empathetic approach to assisting folks to work through conflict. I am fortunate to call Dan a colleague and friend."

Mark Coldren
Leadership & Engagement Specialist, College and University Professional Association for Human Resources (CUPA-HR)
Retired—AVP and CHRO, Human Resources, University at Buffalo, SUNY
Former National Board Chair, CUPA-HR

"As a leader in human resources at a higher-education institution, I can confirm that conflict is prevalent in daily interactions between faculty, staff, and students. The practices asserted in Dan's book are easy to understand and apply to these situations. This will be a useful tool in assisting supervisors and employees with simple tips and strategies to work through everyday interpersonal challenges. Kudos to you, Dan, and thank you for this helpful resource to equip our colleagues in cultivating a collegial workplace."

Chandra Alston, EdD, SPHR, SHRM-SCP, ADC
Vice Chancellor, Human Resources, University of Tennessee Health Science Center

Contents

Introduction
    Every Third Person a Mediator......................... xiii

Chapter 1
    Compassion and Authenticity in Everyday Mediation
    Everyone Has a Bus Story............................... 1

Chapter 2
    First Practice: Recognize the Call
    Develop a Vision for Your Role as Everyday Mediator...... 15

Chapter 3
    Second Practice: Respond in the Moment
    Provide Immediacy and Attention to People in Conflict.... 35

Chapter 4
    Third Practice: Offer a Seat
    Provide a Safe Place to Meet.......................... 55

Chapter 5
    Fourth Practice: Sit with Others
    Create Environments for Talking, Listening,
    and Empathy Amid the Chaos 75

Chapter 6
    Fifth Practice: Share the Ride
    Ceaselessly Support Others Through the
    Long Journey to Reconciliation 105

Chapter 7
    Sixth Practice: Bring Transformative Power
    Find, Support, and Exploit Breakthrough Moments 131

Chapter 8
  Seventh Practice: Support a Dignified Exit
  Conclude with Grace, Dignity, and Respect,
  No Matter the Outcome 163

Chapter 9
  Conclusion: If We're Being Honest with Ourselves
  And That's a Big If. 203

Endnotes 241

Acknowledgments 245

About the Author 247

Introduction

Every Third Person a Mediator

Wherever we look, we see people in conflict. It's a complex world, and we are complex people, each with our own set of experiences, emotions, and expectations that dictate how we interact with others and how we navigate the world. We are experiencing political, economic, social, and cultural upheaval on a global scale and facing conflicts that are seemingly intractable and beyond our comprehension of how, or whether, they will ever be resolved.

Further, whether it is in the workplace, a neighborhood, a classroom, a school hallway, a sports field, a mall, the street, or any other place where people congregate, live, work, travel, and play, there could be a conflict. But large or small, don't all conflicts amount to relationships and how two or more people choose to engage (or not) in order to find common ground?

Sometimes, we can resolve conflicts amicably on our own. Other times, we need a little help. When that happens, wouldn't it be great if a third person were there to skillfully and genuinely help us work through it? What if you were that third person, ready and able to help two others (or more) work through their differences and find common ground in their moment of crisis?

What if every third person were a mediator?

I call these third persons "mediators" for ease of description, but what I am referring to is anyone willing, able, and courageous enough to stand in the fray and use their natural talents and abilities to give people in conflict the time and space to work through their differences. I am not merely talking about the work of "experts," the professional mediators trained to support others in specialized fields. I am talking about each one of us. Though mediation is often seen as something only the experts can do, such as lawyer-mediators helping parties avoid protracted lawsuits, we all have the skills, aptitude, expertise, and gravitas—right now—to be the mediator others need.

This book is based on this premise. Its perspective differs from mediation processes traditionally practiced in the legal system or similarly regulated settings where specially trained mediators are engaged to settle transactional disputes. As invaluable as the service of mediation is, it is not brain surgery, rocket science, or computer coding. Unlike a deficit mindset that assumes that you lack what's needed, my approach builds on your existing abilities, offering guidance to structure your efforts. Mediation is unpredictable and imperfect, but you've likely already developed ways to help others find common ground. No conflict resolves the same way, but as a mediator, your role is to guide the journey—what happens next is up to them. You have the capacity to mediate.

The underlying vision and motivation for this book is found in this context. It is based first on a vision at the individual level—to help you, the everyday person, develop the confidence to tap into your toolbox of interpersonal and human-relations skills and support others as they resolve their conflicts. *This is life-changing.*

Second, it is based on a vision at a global scale: if enough of us are helping at least two others address their conflict in the many spaces and places where there is a need (and there are endless needs), wouldn't the flapping butterfly wings of our efforts contribute to the change we need in the world? *This is world-changing.*

However, to find value in this book, you don't need a broader vision of world change or to worry about how you alone may accomplish that task. Just start with a powerful vision for yourself and how your efforts can change the lives of others. You are the mediator they need—right now—and the work you do matters, greatly. This is a manual and inspirational guide to help you do just that: be the third person in everyday life helping others address their interpersonal conflicts.

This book is for anyone seeking to support others through mediated communication processes—whether you are a friend helping friends (or colleagues or loved ones), a professional in any given field seeking to support colleagues within your organization, or a seasoned mediation professional wanting to support interpersonal communication and relationship dynamics more intentionally in your practice. It is for you, the everyday mediator, to help you address conflicts in the trenches of work, life, and play where we lack the time, resources, and luxury to wait for mediation "experts" to arrive. We are the experts.

Through a long career as an attorney, registered civil mediator, conflict-resolution specialist, and educator—specializing in mediating workplace and higher-education disputes—I have seen the varying extents of both conflicts and the roles each third person can play in helping to resolve them. I have learned that my greatest passion and most valuable professional contribution is to teach others to mediate in everyday contexts. I now share my insights with you. I have known for many years that this is *what* I've wanted to share, but it took a little longer to understand *why*.

Why do I believe that developing ourselves as everyday mediators matters so much to the world? From where is my passion derived?

I believe it stems from my memory of a childhood experience—on a school bus, of all places—that has surfaced quite vividly in recent years. And because of that memory, I now have a deeper understanding of what it means to help others transform their relationships through the journey of mediation. In fact, mediation can be just like a school-bus ride, where you are the compassionate schoolchild helping others find a seat and then navigate a difficult, unsettling, and occasionally terrifying ride to a renewed place of hope and reconciliation. Honing our abilities to be even more effective in mediating conflicts starts with developing the skills, traits, and characteristics necessary for helping others navigate their conflict situations, then applying them to the bumpy journey in a thoughtful way.

This book is my opportunity to share this journey as I board the bus and share the bumpy ride with you. Throughout the following pages, we will revisit the bus ride as a useful metaphor for the many opportunities we have to help others through conflict in the multiple places we live, work, walk, play, ride, and serve. We will further examine the bus ride to understand how conflict develops, progresses, and escalates, along with the baggage, opportunities, fears, and hopes people bring to mediation. We will also look at how we can help them navigate this chaos to gain understanding and perspective, communicate more effectively, and move toward resolution, even reconciliation.

We start in **Chapter 1** with some of the most foundational aspects of mediation—compassion and authenticity—which will be demonstrated in that school-bus story I mentioned. The remaining chapters outline *The Mediation Road Map for the Bumpy Ride to Conflict Resolution*, a thoughtful set of practices for guiding others toward reconciliation. Each practice on the road map corresponds to a chapter as follows:

- **Chapter 2 | First Practice: Recognize the Call; Develop a Vision for Your Role as Everyday Mediator.** The everyday mediators of the world don't wait for someone else to step in. We don't absolve ourselves of responsibility on the uncertain hope that someone else will be available.
- **Chapter 3 | Second Practice: Respond in the Moment; Provide Immediacy and Attention to People in Conflict.** The more we make ourselves available and accessible to others, the more we help them move quickly to resolution and avoid continued angst and escalated tensions.
- **Chapter 4 | Third Practice: Offer a Seat; Provide a Safe Place to Meet.** Conflicts rarely occur in places of peace and solitude. We must not only be immediate but also help others find a safe space as the chaos of work and life swirls around us.
- **Chapter 5 | Fourth Practice: Sit with Others; Create Environments for Talking, Listening, and Empathy Amid the Chaos.** People in conflict can feel confused if they are not given time to simply sit with their issues, with a patient neutral presence there providing the gift of space and time, without interjections or an attempt to fix things their way.
- **Chapter 6 | Fifth Practice: Share the Ride; Ceaselessly Support Others Through the Long Journey to Reconciliation.** Mediators must be neutral and unbiased—and in doing so, we can feel constrained from conveying a deeper connection. We should instead feel comfortable conveying, in effect, that *yes, if your experience is as you say it is (even though I must also appreciate the experience of the other participant whose view may be different), I would also feel the pain that you are expressing.*

- **Chapter 7 | Sixth Practice: Bring Transformative Power; Find, Support, and Exploit Breakthrough Moments.** Participants must make choices about how, or whether, they will resolve their conflict, but mediators serve as catalysts. Our presence transforms one participant's response, breaking down their defenses, which in turn breaks down whatever defenses the other participant is holding onto.
- **Chapter 8 | Seventh Practice: Support a Dignified Exit; Conclude with Grace, Dignity, and Respect, No Matter the Outcome.** All mediations must end. Mediators hope they will end well but can't control what the participants will ultimately decide. They help plan the best conclusion possible. With resolution, they help identify the next steps to ensure that participants honor and fulfill their agreements. With or without resolution, they ensure that their dignity and self-worth remain intact and, as best as possible, offer a glimmer of hope for resolution down the road.

Within each of these chapters—at each stop of the road map—you will find anecdotes, straightforward explanations, and practical insights and examples. We will examine the essential characteristics, skills, and behaviors for being an everyday mediator. Though many are common to traditional mediation practices, others challenge traditional thinking about the purposes mediators serve and roles they play. Each chapter concludes with a reflection tool and exercise you can use or adapt as needed for the everyday conflict situations you face. I conclude in **Chapter 9** with final reflections on the journey to becoming an everyday mediator.

Mediation may not heal every painful experience, but if enough of us become that "every third person" and apply its principles in everyday moments along life's bumpy bus ride, it can make a real difference. Are you ready? It's time to board.

Chapter 1

Compassion and Authenticity in Everyday Mediation

Everyone Has a Bus Story

Mediation may seem like a structured process, but it truly comes to life through the trust, safety, and understanding we breathe into it. Our compassion and authenticity—rooted in our own lived experiences—shape how we guide others through conflict.

It is our past experiences that influence both how we engage with others and the choices we make. They teach us empathy, resilience, and perspective. By reflecting on these moments, we can better understand our own actions and motivations and bring genuine care and presence to mediation. This self-awareness allows us to build trust, create meaningful dialogue, and help participants navigate conflict with greater clarity and connection. And it allows us to build on what has served us well and reframe challenges into opportunities for growth, setting the stage for more meaningful mediation.

A Story: A Gentle Presence—A Quiet Power
I played percussion throughout junior high, high school, and college. One day in junior high, our band performed a concert at a remote location. Since the school didn't have a drum set, I had to use my own. While playing, I unknowingly fell offbeat, throwing the whole performance off. Bill, the first trombone, was quick to blame me afterward. His words stung, but I could not argue with him.

After the concert, percussionists were last to board the bus since we had the most to pack. I managed to store most of my drum set except for the large bass drum, which I had to carry onto the bus with me. As I stepped inside, already feeling depleted, I was hit with a symphony of loud *boos* from my bandmates. It came from every direction and, worst of all, included my close friends, Dave and Kevin. Dave even stood in the aisle, blocking my path, repeatedly pointing at me while chanting "boo!"

Dave was a trombone player and a joker. Whether he was angry like Bill or just entertained by the moment, I didn't know. His expression seemed more amused than malicious, but that didn't lessen the humiliation. My head spun as I stood there, weighed down by my drum and the overwhelming shame. It lasted mere seconds but felt like an eternity.

Then, something in me snapped. I dropped my bass drum and punched Dave hard in the chest. He gasped, stumbled back, and fell into his seat. "Get out of my way!" I shouted.

But the ordeal wasn't over. I had no place to sit. The bus was full, and no one was about to offer me a spot. I stood, shaking, scanning for an escape—until a voice broke through the tension.

"You can sit here."

Michelle, a quiet flute player, stood, gesturing to the empty seat beside her. I tentatively sat down, grateful not to be standing in the aisle with everyone looking at me. In retrospect, what struck me was that she didn't then say much during the ride. She didn't comfort me with words, touch, or distraction. She simply sat, present in my pain. She glanced at me now and then—her expression calm yet full of understanding. She carried no obligation, no personal stake in my humiliation, yet she chose to share in it.

Things improved on the bus. I dreaded leaving my seat next to Michelle, but I had to carry my drum—and my humiliation—off the bus. As I passed, Dave simply said, "Sorry, Dan." Maybe it was the punch, but I'd like to think Michelle's quiet presence played a part. He recognized his mistake and wanted to make amends. I forgave him and Kevin, and we remained friends.

Everyday Mediators
Conflicts and conversations can range from basic misunderstandings to matters of distrust, manipulation, and alienation to the perceptions and realities of racial, gender, and other forms of animus. Sharing these experiences can be painful, revealing, and healing all in one. I have heard too many stories where people not only faced anger, thoughtlessness, ignorance, intolerance, harsh judgment, negativity, and hate but also endured those experiences alone. They never received the opportunity for redress or to process their experiences and find meaning and healing—not in the moment, not within a few days or weeks, perhaps not in their lifetime. They had no mediator. They had no Michelle.

Now consider: what if every third seat on the bus or plane had a Michelle? What if every office suite had a Michelle or every third house in the neighborhood, third pew in church, or third seat at the theater? What if every third passenger, pedestrian, driver, customer, employee, leader, team member, or person in any other walk of life were a Michelle? What if you were Michelle?

We are also grateful when there is a Michelle on board, able to live in the chaos and help us live there as well. You can play that role too. I apply this story to mediation because it is during everyday times in everyday places where we, typically the third person, are needed most and needed now to help two others (or more) work through their conflicts. The question is whether you see that role for yourself as an everyday mediator and choose to offer others a seat, sit with them, and experience together the difficult ride on whatever bus you boarded today.

When we think of our own school-bus stories, I hope that we can all remember the mediators (although we likely never called them that)—the ones who disrupted bullies from bullying further. The ones who stood between the weak and the strong. The ones who offered losers a seat, sat with them, and let them cry or complain or ramble senselessly. The ones who took the taunts meant for others. The ones who tried to help arguing friends reconcile. The ones who tried to bring order, reason, and calm amid the chaos. And all this as the bus lumbered down the bumpy road.

They are the ones who find ways—magically, innately, by trial and error—to bring peace and calm to messy situations. They don't solve problems; they facilitate opportunities for others to solve problems for themselves. When they don't help bring peace or turn combatants to lasting friends, they at least provide space for others to think differently about their actions and have the opportunity to find resolution somewhere down the road.

So how do they do that? With compassion, and with authenticity.

The Role of Compassion in Everyday Mediators

My school-bus story represents the tip of the iceberg of the many unexpected ways compassion reveals itself in everyday mediation. Though she wasn't a mediator in the traditional sense, Michelle's example illustrates what is at the heart of being a truly effective mediator who connects with, and is present for, others. That quiet power she demonstrated was compassion. She didn't need to say, "It's okay." Instead, her unspoken message was clear: "You're not alone. We'll get through this together."

On that day on the bus, I felt ambushed and terrified yet received grace, compassion, and mercy at the precise moment I needed it. Ever since, I have experienced times when I felt scared, confused, and alone and looked for someone like Michelle but could not find her. I found no compassion in my office or in my work circumstances—which I believe is how too many people feel too often every day, at work and elsewhere. There are simply not enough Michelles to go around.

I have shared this story and connected with many others through it in facilitating mediations and dialogue processes to help individuals and groups work through conflict situations. I've learned that everyone has a bus story, and many don't end well. It would always make me think: *What might have happened if I'd had no Michelle that day? What if, after I'd punched Dave and struggled down the aisle with my drum, I'd found no seat?*

Without a mediator on the bus (without Michelle), I may have acted quite differently. If the *boos* persisted, if someone nearby continued to tease, to hell with the expensive bass drum bought with my parents' hard-earned money!

It would now be a busted, splintered mess as it becomes a battering ram or is heaved over the seat toward my nemesis. I punch the next kid and the next kid who provokes me, or who may now be trying to restrain me. I scream bloody murder. Mayhem ensues. The bus stops, the driver comes back, restrains me, and brings me up front where I sit alone. The ride continues toward school, where I face discipline and an uncertain future—bad enough from the principal, worse from my parents, worse still in juvenile detention like others I have known who received no grace.

How Compassion Shows Up in the Everyday Mediator
Consider your own experiences. Who offered you a seat during conflict? Did they listen fully and without judgment? How did you know that you mattered and that, regardless of your role in the conflict or mistakes you made, you could feel safe, understood, and supported?

Or did compassion manifest in a more surprising way? Did the person confront you and tell you with little subtlety that you're blowing it? Did you stay and listen because you recognized the truth, as much as it pained you to do so? Perhaps the other person angered you and this feeling lingered, but later you saw the actions as a generous gift that was life-changing, maybe even lifesaving.

Or did someone show compassion in a dogged determination not to give up on you? Perhaps they used words and actions that appeared awkward, or with poor timing, or confidence lacking. Maybe they showed some irritation, but you weren't the easiest person to get along with, and you said some hurtful things. You gave no good reason for them to care for you. Yet they did, despite your lack of gratitude, and you got through the struggle based on nothing more than their ceaseless love for you.

Who is to say a gruff, cussing, hard-working union guy isn't showing compassion when he strong-arms two other gruff, cussing, hard-working union guys to sit down over beer after work to talk through their differences in their usual gruff, cussing way? Why should we be surprised when a diminutive, soft-spoken HR representative enters a room with two angry, generally loud employees with seemingly intractable differences and, through firm and tireless insistence on basic ground rules for listening, exits with two calmer, more agreeable coworkers prepared to forge a more cooperative relationship?

The context of the conflict, who you are, who the participants are, your character and demeanor, the judgments you make, and your general manner of interacting with others are among the many variables that influence how you demonstrate compassion. As a compassionate mediator, you are:

- **Patient and calm.** Compassionate mediators provide a calming presence that helps slow the conflict-resolution process down and gives time for participants to explore their challenges fully.
- **Empathetic.** The compassionate mediator demonstrates a deep level of listening to the point where the participants truly feel that you understand where they are coming from. You model empathy so one participant can learn to do the same for the other and in turn begin to experience the other person's empathy for them.
- **Nonjudgmental.** A compassionate mediator isn't a finger-wagger or the judge or jury of others' faults. You won't excuse their behaviors, but you will help them honestly acknowledge those behaviors and how they have gotten in the way so they can learn and move forward with more constructive behaviors and better responses.
- **Encouraging and hopeful.** Compassionate mediators don't admit defeat easily and continue to believe in others and possibilities for resolution perhaps beyond what is reasonable. You offer encouragement and hope to your last dying breath.
- **Tireless and exhaustive.** By being hopeful, compassionate mediators work ceaselessly until resolution is achieved, however distant the prospect.

You look for glimmers of agreement to build upon and treat small concessions as great victories.
- **Appropriately confrontational.** Compassionate mediators balance firmness and compassion. You address misbehavior directly, setting limits on belligerence while guiding others toward cooperation. At the same time, you gently encourage passive individuals to engage, knowing that staying silent can be just as self-defeating. Whether firm or gentle, your goal is always to foster growth and resolution.

Examine the Humanness in Yourself and Others

Maybe you are wondering how far we must go in extending compassion to others. What if we don't like a participant? What if, by all measures of objective reasoning, the person isn't likeable? What if they are bad, misguided, unfair, self-centered, or wrong (among many possible labels)?

We can intellectually grasp concepts around compassion, caring, and genuineness and become smug about how we see ourselves as the go-to person for mediation. But then a situation arises and makes us question whether we actually do possess these qualities at all. We must then dig deep into our well and see the human in the other person—and the imperfect human in ourselves.

Turning to my bus story, perhaps Michelle didn't particularly like me or think much about me up to the point of our encounter. Perhaps she was in general agreement with the others that I had royally messed up during the band recital. But liking me or judging my flaws wasn't part of her calculus. Her decision to help was based on an identified need (my distress), a desire to help, and an innate sense that she had the capacity to help.

We each have a unique lens on the world. If we are not careful, we can come to believe that, because it has served us well, that lens must be accurate in its interpretation of the world and how others should act, behave, and think. Then, when others act, behave, and express perspectives contrary to our own, we think there must be something inaccurate, out of place, or simply wrong with their lens.

However, everyone's lens is inherently untrustworthy and myopic. Is that lens legitimate or does it present barriers that keep us from mediating certain situations in a fair, impartial manner? Or can we address and overcome our distorted lens, allowing us to mediate for individuals whose lenses are vastly different from our own? Understanding this means developing genuineness and authenticity and acknowledging our humanness by exploring the distortions that limit our view.

Being You—Genuineness and Authenticity

Consider the times when you feel most compassionate. This is not the fake variety where, for example, you are at the funeral of a deceased neighbor and express public sympathy toward the widow with whom you were never close—and then think to yourself as you drive home, "I never liked them. I wonder if this means she'll move." She may graciously acknowledge your sense of obligation in attending but will later think, while the movers load her final possessions and she looks one last time at the privacy fence you erected years ago that starved her prize hydrangeas of sunlight, "He never really cared for us."

When you feel true compassion, you clean your internal filters. You are honest with yourself and your emotions and responses and are therefore able to be honest and genuine with others. Your outpouring of concern is natural, instinctual, free-flowing—and thoughtless in the sense that you need no labored contemplation before acting. When truly vested in helping, others see how your compassion and caring, even if awkwardly expressed, comes from a genuine, authentic desire to help.

Traits of Authentic Mediators
Genuine, authentic mediators are:

- **Vulnerable.** Mediators are expected to be competent, but that doesn't mean they won't make mistakes or feel stuck. The ego-driven avoid admitting uncertainty, but true strength lies in openness. A mediator might say, "I'm not sure where to go next—let's take a break," or acknowledge a distraction before refocusing.
- **Comfortable with themselves.** Mediators who can laugh at their mistakes—whether mixing up names or telling a self-deprecating story—create relatability. Humor, humility, and self-acceptance help put participants at ease and foster trust.
- **Thin-skinned toward others' experiences.** Compassionate mediators are attuned to others' struggles, conveying understanding through listening and presence. They don't over-display emotion but also don't shy away from tenderness when addressing painful topics.
- **Thick-skinned when attacked.** Some participants will deflect responsibility by blaming the mediator. Authentic mediators accept that undeserved blame is part of the job and remain unfazed when it happens.
- **Comfortable with conflict.** Mediators don't expect their presence alone to resolve dysfunction. Though they set ground rules, they also understand that high

emotions, arguments, and interruptions can be not only part of the process but actually necessary for real concerns to emerge.
- **Not seeking recognition.** Mediation is often a thankless job. Though success comes from participants' efforts, mediators take quiet satisfaction in guiding them to resolution, knowing they've made an impact even if it goes unrecognized.

What matters most is what you do to help participants achieve whatever outcome they are prepared to achieve at whatever level they are prepared to engage. They simply wish to negotiate a settlement in order to avoid litigation and the necessity of interaction with each other in the future? So be it. They have deep relationship pain and would benefit from exploring the root causes of their conflict? So be it. Whatever the setting or circumstance, be encouraged to bring your innate capacities and develop new capacities for compassion and caring to whatever mediation you find yourself in.

We can all consider Michelle's example and find opportunities for stretching and challenging ourselves to bring our true humanity into the frame. This may mean unlearning what we thought mediation is about and learning new practices, skills, and attitudes that will serve us through this new lens of compassion and authenticity.

We start here because, no matter how many skills you acquire, the foundation of effective mediation is simple: be kind, and be yourself. If you can do that, you've already done more than most. Trust, connection, and humility will carry you forward, even as you fumble and learn along the way. Mediation is a journey, and like any journey, it begins with recognizing the call—our first stop following *The Mediation Road Map for the Bumpy Ride to Conflict Resolution*.

Chapter 1 Reflective Exercise

Journal Prompts for Developing as an Authentic, Everyday Mediator

This projection exercise offers insight into how you view yourself and others, challenging you to recognize whether traits that bother you in others are ones you also possess but rationalize differently. It helps assess your capacity for genuineness, compassion, and self-awareness in mediation, especially with those who "push your buttons." This is not about judgment but growth—understanding your biases and limitations allows you to better serve others and engage with honesty and vulnerability, reflecting on your true self rather than an idealized mediator. By recognizing our shared humanness, we can transcend biases—or, when we can't, step back and ensure fair mediation.

    Reflect on the following prompts based on how you view yourself day to day, not how you believe a compassionate, caring mediator *should* act, behave, and think. Seek honest self-reflection without filters. You will get the most out of this activity if you are vulnerable and open, even if some of the revelations aren't pretty. Also, please refer to the example I provide in the resources section at the end of this book.

1. Respond to the following prompts:
    A. What are the positive traits, characteristics, and qualities you currently possess and want to offer to the world? What makes you you?
    B. What are the unflattering or less-than-positive traits, characteristics, and qualities of individuals that annoy you or push your buttons? Remember to be completely honest—don't hold back.

C. What are the traits, characteristics, and qualities of the person you aspire to be? These are qualities you don't currently possess or don't possess in full measure that you want to develop. If helpful, consider qualities of individuals you admire that you want to emulate.

2. This next step requires serious introspection. Look at what you've written and compare your responses to A and C with your responses to B. Note words and phrases in A, B, and C that are similar in some way. Stretch your thinking to see these similarities, particularly in B, even if the connections seem remote. For example, perhaps the "pushy," "manipulative" person I describe in the resources section behaves that way to accomplish meaningful goals, which I describe more nobly for myself as a "singular focus," commitment to "high standards," and "quality in all areas of life." Also note words or phrases for which you cannot fairly make such connections or for which words and phrases in A and C are clearly different from B. In my example, my annoying person's insecurity, self-indulgence, and efforts to "influence outcomes unfairly" doesn't match my desire to emulate leaders who are "self-assured" and "lead with humility."

3. Reflect on what this means for you. Stretch yourself and consider whether the positive traits, characteristics, and qualities you see in yourself (A), and/or for which you aspire (C), may in any way relate to the negative traits, characteristics, and qualities of individuals who annoy you (B). Is it possible that how they lead their lives, navigate the world, and seek to satisfy their needs are simply their way of doing exactly what you are doing? True, you've undoubtedly identified qualities in B that are beyond excuse and don't even hint at who you are or how you behave. For the rest, perhaps what annoys you about these individuals is that you don't want to see these same qualities in yourself. You don't want to see their humanness and the possibility that they have similar goals, aspirations, and desires as you do, only expressed in ways that you don't want to acknowledge in yourself.

Take time to jot some notes or journal what this exercise means for you and what conclusions you might draw with respect to how you view others and how you seek to support others (or don't).

    Given what you have written:

- When can you transcend your distortions and biases to help others, even those who tend to annoy you?
- When should you be careful and step aside because you can't fairly transcend your reservations?

Continue to write notes and journal on these reflections. Talk with trusted colleagues and others about these issues with the spirit of openness and continued learning and growth while avoiding harsh self-criticism.

Chapter 2

First Practice: Recognize the Call

Develop a Vision for Your Role as Everyday Mediator

"Where there's a need, I'll be there."

Chapter Goals

By the end of this chapter, you will:

- gain a deeper vision for how you can serve as an everyday mediator,
- understand the many opportunities to mediate, and
- be cognizant of some external and internal limitations.

Something happened today. Someone is uncomfortable or upset about something or someone. Or perhaps circumstances have developed in the last few days or weeks where someone is having difficulty relating to someone else, or two people or a small group are struggling to communicate and work together.

Patterns of discomfort, tension, miscommunication, or outright anger can form among people with whom you work, live, play, serve, sit together, or share a ride. The issues and concerns underlying the struggle may be large or small, significant or trivial, consequential to many or just a few. You may be part of the problem, or at least perceived as such, or your involvement may be tangential. You don't have to be a mediation expert to recognize the role you can play.

The sad truth is that many people fail to see the role they can play in resolving someone else's conflict—but you will, and because of that, you will have taken the first practice in being an everyday mediator. You will have recognized the call.

A Story: "Recognize the Call" in Action

Carla, an HR executive, looked forward to attending the local HR conference on Monday. It was an opportunity to get away from the office, learn something new, network, and put aside the pressures of work for a while. Her colleagues Amanda and Brian would also be attending.

Last week was busy. Amanda and Brian worked diligently on a big report about compensation and pay equity, for which Amanda was the data specialist and Brian wrote the narrative. Amanda spent a lot of time crunching numbers and discussing them with Brian. Brian then wrote several drafts that interpreted the data. They submitted the report to Denise, the organization's HR director. Denise shared the report with executive leadership, who were quite pleased and complimentary to both Amanda and Brian for their efforts.

Carla was not involved in this project but was certainly aware of the hard work Amanda and Brian put into it. Carla works in employee relations where, among other duties, she helps employees, managers, and teams work through conflict situations using mediation processes. However, she had never had to help colleagues in her own department resolve a conflict.

Friday, the HR team attended a routine monthly meeting with colleagues from the finance and administration division. These meetings cover a broad range of topics

First Practice: Recognize the Call

involving HR policies and practices along with budgetary and operational issues. The finance team also complimented Brian and Amanda on their report and asked questions about their methodology. Amanda started to explain, but Brian interrupted and took over the conversation from there. Amanda then remained quiet for the rest of the meeting and left quickly afterward. Friday meetings usually ended with idle chat about everyone's weekend plans, but this time, Amanda was noticeably absent.

Carla had forgotten about Friday's meeting when she sat down Monday morning with Brian and Amanda in the large conference room prior to the morning keynote. Brian was friendly and gregarious. Amanda was polite but unusually reserved.

Brian inquired, "How are you, Amanda? How was your weekend?"

Amanda answered curtly, "Why should you care?"

"What do you mean?" asked Brian, to which Amanda responded with complaints about the report and Brian's behavior at the meeting.

Brian interrupted, "Get over yourself, Amanda."

Carla's heart sank. She considered excusing herself and leaving them to their own devices. She thought: *Why should I care? Their private little spat has no bearing on my life. Or does it?* Her next thought was to suggest that she join them in the lobby to talk out the situation. They might miss the keynote but would have a chance to repair their relationship and enjoy the conference afterward.

A Deeper Vision: How You Can Serve as an Everyday Mediator

Conflicts and skirmishes surface continually when and in spaces where we least expect them. We will find ourselves thrust into sudden opportunities to serve as intermediaries, just like Carla had. Now, of course, she possessed mediation skills as part of her professional role, but this situation involved a different context than the usual pre-arranged mediation meetings she facilitated. This matter was more personal as it involved colleagues with whom she worked closely. She had a choice not to get involved but instead, recognizing the need and finding herself involuntarily brought into the conflict, she realized that she played a role and had the capacity to help. She chose to sacrifice her immediate personal interests to offer support.

Similar to Carla, visualizing yourself as a mediator will guide you to respond as needed to keep people in conflict civil and respectful as they bump into one another and find reasons to argue. Let's consider how the mediator in you surfaces in various walks of life:

- **Manager or team leader.** Conflict is natural within teams, often arising from work issues, personality differences, or employee responsibilities. Though you may not always be neutral, you can apply mediation skills—listening, encouraging dialogue, and guiding decisions—to help resolve conflicts before intervention is needed.
- **Team member or peer.** As a peer, mediation comes naturally since you share equal standing with colleagues. If team members turn to you for support, you can offer calm guidance, helping them navigate interpersonal conflicts and fostering better collaboration.
- **Institutional representative.** HR, equity, and employee-relations professionals frequently use mediation skills. Some organizations provide mediation before formal disciplinary processes,

whereas others rely on informal conflict resolution to improve communication and workplace interactions.
- **Service professional.** Whether behind a counter or in a high-stakes environment, you encounter daily opportunities to de-escalate conflicts. From customer-service disputes to patient advocacy, social work, and law enforcement, mediation helps maintain order and resolve misunderstandings in all sorts of service roles.
- **Friend, family member, or neighbor.** You may not always be seen as neutral. In fact, you may be in the thick of the drama. Yet there is no reason you can't refine your approach to interject skills, strategies, and ideas as a mediator would to help you and your friends, neighbors, and loved ones work through issues more productively than you have in the past.

Embrace a World of Plenty (of Opportunities to Mediate)

It's time to expand your mindset even further about the endless places and spaces where people in conflict could benefit from your assistance. Not all opportunities will involve a formal sit-down where you announce yourself as "mediator." Many may be found through the informal mediator-type roles you play in your daily life. You have a world of possibilities and must be prepared to respond when opportunities arise. To help clarify those possibilities, the following provides answers to some of the most common questions I've encountered when teaching and guiding others to develop as mediators:

Q. The world is a dark place. Is mediation really a panacea for all the world's conflicts?

A. Mediation may not be the first line of defense for addressing some of our deepest, darkest, and seemingly intractable conflicts, but opportunities far outweigh situations where mediation is not viable. People of good intention, strong will, and a sense of justice can and will overcome such conflicts. Our efforts also reduce the prevalence of unproductive conflict arising in the first place. Embrace this and you need not worry about opportunities for facilitating change in the world through mediation.

Q. What are some of the processes everyday mediators and other third-party interveners use?

A. The mere presence of a third party can influence how individuals in conflict interact, often helping them find a means for working toward a resolution that they were unable to achieve on their own. As these efforts progress toward de-escalation, or even just nudge slightly that way, mediation and other third-party processes can help provide pathways to resolution. These include the following:

- Coaching others to address conflicts on their own
- Advocating for forums and fair processes that ensure that individuals in conflict are fully heard
- Teaching concepts, tools, and strategies for problem-solving, collaboration, and nonviolent intervention
- Speaking out against systemic injustice
- Serving as a bystander to witness and intervene in support of others
- Serving behind the scenes to provide resources and advise others of their rights

Q. I don't see the prevalence of everyday conflict in my world. Am I missing something?

A. If you don't feel that conflict is a significant concern in your world, consider yourself fortunate. However, conflict is there—just not always in a bad way—as, when managed effectively, it can lead to collaborative, synergistic outcomes. Though some people navigate disputes maturely without the need for outside help, many existing conflict-resolution processes are structured more for formal adjudication than meaningful resolution.

Mediation is a form of "alternative dispute resolution," but "alternative" to what? Like arbitration and neutral case evaluation, it is an alternative to litigation. Though welcome, the term "alternative" implies that adjudication in some form remains the default and perhaps preferred mechanism for managing disputes. That's because mediation and other alternative dispute-resolution methods are often treated as afterthoughts rather than primary tools for addressing disputes.

This dynamic is mirrored in workplace settings, where grievance processes often replicate legal-system patterns, escalating issues to third-party decisions rather than allowing for resolution between the parties involved. Though some organizations incorporate mediation before disputes escalate, many employees struggle to find informal avenues for resolution, leading them to file grievances as their only option.

For healthier work environments and communities, early-intervention mediation and proactive conflict-resolution practices should be prioritized, giving individuals the tools to address disputes before they escalate and thus a chance to restore the relationship.

Q. I don't want to be a busybody. Shouldn't we just let people work out their conflicts on their own? Why should I care? Why should I get involved?

A. Being a busybody implies getting into people's business, even if your relationship with them is remote or nonexistent. *Introverts like me don't do that!* I'm not advocating for a do-gooder mentality that says, in effect, "I'm a mediator, and I'm here to help." For many life situations, if you are a trusted friend, colleague, family member, neighbor, or community member, or you serve in other roles that connect you with people in the same environment, you will respond when the need arises.

I haven't always stepped up when I knew I could have. I've been uncaring, uncertain, or simply scared. I'm not proud of that, but I'm human. If you believe in the value of being that third person helping two others resolve their conflict, you will accept the challenge when you can. You may miss some opportunities, but your desire and, over time, confidence and skill will guide you to make these small but vital contributions. That's not being a busybody. It's being noble and modest.

Q. I'm not sure I have the expertise and credibility I need to be a mediator. How can I be accepted as a credible mediator without more education and experience?

A. Traditional forms of mediation, such as those regulated through the legal system, require a different form of expertise and credibility than do other forms, such as the model I present in this book. Though mediators in the legal profession and other defined fields provide invaluable service to support resolution to avoid more protracted and costly court battles, these processes are often transactional and do not delve into deeper interpersonal relationship concerns.

Whether you aspire to be a professional mediator or simply to fortify existing skills and roles, this framework builds on the innate skills you already possess to address everyday conflicts.

Be Aware of Limitations

Mediation should help parties resolve their issues; however, attempts to mediate under the wrong circumstances can actually make matters worse. As such, there are situations where mediation should be avoided, which fall into two broad categories: (1) where mediation is generally inappropriate because of external factors and (2) where mediation may be appropriate but you are not the most appropriate mediator because of internal factors.[1]

External Factors

Certain situations—such as those involving coercion, extreme power imbalance, threats, ongoing abuse, or a lack of good faith—can make mediation ineffective or even harmful. Safety must always come first, and if participants feel coerced or unable to speak freely, the process loses its integrity. Additionally, legal or organizational restrictions may limit when mediation is appropriate. Recognizing these limits is essential to ensuring fair, effective conflict resolution. Mediation is generally not appropriate when the following are true:

- **The process is not voluntary.** Mediation must allow participants to make choices about the process, including whether to engage at all. Though some may reluctantly agree, coercion—such as forcing mediation under threat of discipline—compromises its voluntary nature.
- **Power differentials can't be overcome.** Mediation often involves imbalances in financial, social, or

organizational power. Though these disparities can't be eliminated, mediation can still proceed when the more powerful party is open to discussion, even if they remain skeptical.
- **Risk of further trauma.** Mediation should not be used when it risks re-traumatizing a participant, such as in cases of bullying. Restorative models, such as victim-offender mediation, occur only after wrongdoing has been established and focus on acknowledgment and amends rather than equal negotiation.
- **Legal or policy restrictions.** Certain cases, such as criminal matters or workplace misconduct involving harassment, are often excluded from mediation due to policies that prioritize accountability and protection over negotiation.
- **Safety concerns.** If there is a risk of physical harm, whether apparent from the start or emerging during mediation, the process must be immediately halted in order to ensure safety.
- **Mediation is unethical.** Like the physician's code, mediators should "first, do no harm." Along with the situations already discussed, ethical considerations preclude mediation when the following occurs:

    ○ A participant never intended to consider a mediated outcome and instead uses the opportunity to build a case against the other. For example, mediation should not continue when it becomes evident that a manager's apparent willingness to participate is actually a ruse to learn more about an employee's culpability to impose discipline later.
    ○ Mediation is used to impose adverse action. Though having a third party in the room is

acceptable for disciplinary action, it should not be called mediation when participants lack true options in decisions affecting them. Use your best mediation skills but be clear about your true purpose.

- **Risk to confidentiality.** A mediator should not share details of discussions, even with a leader who has initiated the mediation. Insightful leaders respect confidentiality and focus on outcomes rather than the specifics of conversations.
- **Limits to confidentiality.** If legal or policy violations, such as sexual misconduct, are revealed, mediation cannot continue, and the mediator may be required to report the issue. In such cases, participants should be informed and appropriate referrals should be made.
- **Unethical or illegal agreements.** Mediation must not proceed if proposed terms involve breaking laws, violating company policies, or exploiting a weaker party into accepting unfair or unethical conditions.

Internal Factors

Everyday mediators, such as friends helping friends, do not have the constraints of professional mediators. But that doesn't mean they aren't innately guided by standards of fairness, objectivity, credibility, and trust to effectively support others. They act intuitively to provide the proper support in helping others reach a resolution as both a neutral and impartial third party.

Neutrality
Despite your desire to help others resolve a conflict, you should not mediate if you can't do so fairly and objectively.

This includes situations where even if you see no barrier to mediating, one or more participants may. Whether mediating professionally or more informally, we must observe and respect these parameters to support participants in the resolution of their conflict.

Everyday mediators must conduct themselves in a neutral, impartial manner. We do not take sides, and our actions and words must not convey that we favor or believe one side over another. We should not express our opinion about the merits or worth of a participant's case or situation. We must ensure that both sides (and all sides in multi-party disputes) are fully heard and considered during deliberations. We should also seek to balance the relative participation of each participant, including time to talk, time to listen, opportunity to be fully heard, and so forth. For example, a participant may question your neutrality if you spend most of your time ensuring that the other participant has the opportunity to express concerns and then limit this opportunity for them.

Ensuring neutrality is a matter of judgment. Generally, if you continually check in with the participants to ensure that they feel fully heard, allow them to challenge you at any point when they feel you may not be acting in a neutral fashion, and then seek to address such concerns, you are demonstrating your genuine intent to remain neutral.

Impartiality

Whereas neutrality relates to your actions and behaviors, impartiality relates to what you believe and whether your beliefs will affect your ability to mediate fairly and objectively. Do you have a bias about the issues in dispute or about either or both participants that will prevent you from mediating?

Perhaps specific issues challenge your values beyond your ability to maintain a neutral stance. This may include profound religious, ethical, political, social, or moral values on such issues as abortion, sexual relationships, marriage, race relations, or any viewpoint or perspective that you strongly oppose. Perhaps your reservations are more pedestrian. Does a person's apparent prejudice about equality in the workplace, views on people of a different gender, race, or sexual orientation, or stated or implicit value system contrast so markedly from your own that you can't imagine giving them a fair shot?

If a dispute challenges your core values—religious, ethical, political, or social—it may be difficult to remain impartial. Strong biases, whether against or for a participant, can cloud your judgment. If you find yourself wanting to advocate rather than mediate, or if a participant's views make fair treatment impossible, you should step aside. Impartiality is key; if you can't remain objective, you shouldn't mediate.

Other Reasons You May Not Be the Appropriate Mediator

Beyond concerns about neutrality and impartiality, there are other reasons you may not be the appropriate mediator for a particular conflict. For example, consider the following questions:

1. **Do you have the right skills and experience?** Though many mediations don't require expertise, some may be too emotionally charged or complex for your comfort level. Factors such as lack of technical knowledge, multi-party dynamics, or unfamiliar relationships may preclude you from mediation.
2. **Are you being pressured to mediate to a predetermined outcome?** If an authority figure implies that mediation should lead to a specific result, it means you're being asked to manipulate the process. In such cases, you should always remove yourself from the situation.

3. Do power imbalances make you uncomfortable? Ethical concerns arise when mediation is misused for personal gain. If you lack confidence in handling such complexities, it's best to step aside.

If you decide that you are not the appropriate mediator, you can still help participants identify someone else, if possible. Perhaps others within your organization can mediate or you can refer the participants to other mediators in the community or a professional mediation service. However, if your only barrier is a perceived lack of expertise, confidence, or skills to mediate on your own, consider finding a more seasoned mediator with whom you can co-mediate. Doing so is a great way to learn and develop rather than withdraw and end up missing the opportunity.

The Duty to Disclose—You Don't Have to Be Perfect
Talk of neutrality and impartiality can suggest that, unless your mind is blank and the participants and their issues are foreign to you, you cannot mediate. This is not so. If it were, no one could mediate. Instead, you must recognize potential concerns and address them appropriately. This is the duty to disclose, but it may or may not mean you must withdraw from serving as mediator.

Decisions about what to disclose involve matters of judgment. You may have doubts about particular comments made, proposals offered, or the merits of one side's arguments over the other's. You may have value judgments about one participant's statements, manner, ethics, or morals. You do not need to search your conscience for every possible reservation. If you don't view these matters as serious and can commit to giving all participants the full opportunity to pursue their interests, you can serve as mediator, imperfect though you are. It works like this:

1. **Identify potential issues that may influence your ability to mediate fairly, objectively, and impartially.**

2. **Determine for yourself whether you can overcome these issues to provide appropriate support. If not, you should withdraw and, ideally, help find another mediator.**

3. **Even if you have no concerns, disclose and fully vet the following with the participants:**

- Your prior or existing relationship with each participant, including the nature of that relationship and any circumstance that may suggest a concern about favoring one participant or their interests over another. For example, you previously worked on the same team as one of the participants, you were a participant's manager, or a participant was your manager. Or you run into one another in the hallway or outside work, have lunch together, or engage in idle chitchat with enough frequency that the other participant could reasonably have concerns.
- Your prior or existing involvement with the underlying issues or prior knowledge about any aspect of the dispute that may impact deliberations. For example, in your current or prior role, you were aware of issues underlying the dispute and perhaps offered advice to a participant about how to address the matter.
- Any relevant details about your background and experience that may suggest a bias for or against a particular issue under dispute. For example, the participants are researchers in a lab that does stem-cell research, which you oppose, but you believe that fact won't prevent you from helping the participants resolve their differences. Or you are a staunch supporter of private-school vouchers and are asked

to mediate a dispute among members of a public-school board who are arguing about how to respond to growing political pressure to support vouchers.

4. Explain how you feel that the matters you have disclosed shouldn't impact your ability to fairly and objectively mediate.

5. Answer participants' questions and ask them if they have any concerns. If there are no concerns, proceed with mediation. If there are concerns you are unable to address, withdraw.

How We Recognize the Call

This is how we recognize the call—by realizing that mediation isn't just a formal process but rather a role we naturally step into as we help others navigate conflict, communicate better, and find resolution. President Jimmy Carter, who facilitated the Camp David Accords between Israel and Egypt, probably never viewed himself as an everyday mediator. But there may not be anyone who by grit, intuition, passion, proximity, and authority better embodied an "in the moment" everyday mediator and demonstrated what is possible in such a role. You may not call yourself a mediator, but acknowledging and embracing this role allows you to refine your skills and apply them with intention. In Carter's words, "I have one life and one chance to make it count for something … my faith demands that I do whatever I can, wherever I am, whenever I can, for as long as I can, with whatever I have, to try to make a difference."[2]

The world is full of "whatevers" and "wherevers." You experience this every day, *whatever* the issue is and *wherever* people need help to communicate better, fight better, and work through differences so they have a chance at better relationships and ways of working and living together. You must then be open to possibilities and prepared to respond wherever and whenever they arise. Though your wherevers may not involve overly dramatic conflicts and certainly not physical altercations, your skills and experiences will lend vital support for people in any conflict. Thinking this way should greatly expand your universe of opportunities for recognizing the call to serve as an everyday mediator. The world needs what you have to offer as an everyday mediator. Now it's time to respond in the moment—embrace the opportunities, prepare, and step forward with confidence.

Chapter 2 Reflective Exercise

Discover Your Mediation Wherevers

What are your mediation wherevers? Consider the many roles you play and, for each, brainstorm all the possible relationships and situations for which there are or could be conflicts. Consider relationships and situations that may lack an apparent conflict but where your mediator skills could still be useful. Be exhaustive. There are more wherevers than may be immediately apparent. For an example, please see the resources section at the end of the book.

My Mediation "Wherevers"

Role (Describe)	Relationships and Situations (Current or Potential) Where Mediation Skills Will Be Useful
Manager or Team Leader:	
Team Member or Peer:	
Institutional Representative:	

First Practice: Recognize the Call

Service Professional:	
Friend, Family Member, or Neighbor:	
Good Person on Bus (or Elsewhere):	
Other:	

Chapter 3

Second Practice: Respond in the Moment

Provide Immediacy and Attention to People in Conflict

"I wonder...perhaps I can help."

Chapter Goals

By the end of this chapter, you will:

- understand how to be vigilant for opportunities to support others through mediation,
- be ready to engage in processes for bringing people to the table, and
- recognize and respond to resistance to mediation.

After you recognize the call, there will come a moment when you must respond to support others in conflict. Matters that escalate quickly and are overtly disruptive probably require immediate attention. Matters that simmer may not require immediate support, often because the people in conflict deserve the chance to resolve matters on their own. Instinct, as much as practice and experience, will help you recognize those moments when others could use a hand to work through their differences.

Everyday mediators are close to the action and just an office, cubicle, short walk, or phone call away. Perhaps you work closely with the individuals in conflict as their manager, team leader, or coworker, or you routinely support them in such moments in your capacity as HR, institutional equity, or employee-relations representative. Perhaps you are a friend, family member, neighbor, volunteer, or fellow member of a board, community or church group, nonprofit, sports team, or other group where people assemble and experience moments of conflict.

Responding in the moment means you stand ready to jump in when these moments arise, encourage others to consider a different path, and serve as their guide.

A Story: "Respond in the Moment" in Action

Jo, the office manager of a nonprofit that retrains displaced workers, had worked with Ben, the agency's warm and passionate executive director, for over a decade. He empowered Jo to run daily operations while he focused on partnerships and fundraising. Two years ago, Jo hired Ashley, a spirited but sometimes distracted office coordinator. The three worked well together—until Ben's sudden death.

Jo held things together as the board searched for a new director. Ashley, devastated, struggled to stay on track, and Jo coached her through. When Kim, an MBA-trained executive with no industry experience, took over, tensions rose. Lacking Ben's warmth, Kim relied on Jo but clashed with Ashley. When Kim took over Ashley's supervision, patience wore thin. Ashley's weekly meetings with Kim became increasingly tense.

One morning, Kim called Jo and Ashley into the conference room. She relayed a tech firm's complaints about their service since Ben's passing and outlined tasks to mend the relationship.

Ashley bristled. "How will this actually fix the problem?" she pressed.

Second Practice: Respond in the Moment

Kim sighed. "Ashley, I just need you to help us keep this account."

Ashley snapped. "You spend all your time telling me what I do wrong, but I don't see you doing a damn thing."

Jo tensed.

Kim's voice hardened. "We aren't here to talk about me. I'm just asking you to—"

"Don't blame me. They don't trust you. You're not Ben."

"Ashley," Jo warned, placing a hand on the table.

Kim hesitated and then, to Jo's surprise, her voice cracked. "I'm just trying to keep this place going." Tears welled in her eyes. "I'm—"

Ashley stood abruptly. "I'm done." She stormed out.

Kim wiped her face. "I'm sorry. That was unprofessional." She hesitated, then admitted, "The tech-firm conversation was rough. And my daughter's school refuses to provide the support she needs—her behaviors are getting worse."

Jo took this in. Kim was human after all. "Do you want me to get Ashley?"

Kim shook her head. "It won't do any good. I really was trying to help her."

Jo found Ashley furiously typing. "That was uncalled for," Jo said gently.

"I don't care. I've had it," replied Ashley.

"I don't think you have the full picture."

Ashley scoffed. "What, because she cried? She criticizes me and then melts down?"

Jo sat silently. Ashley exhaled and admitted that she missed Ben. "This place isn't the same."

"I know," Jo said. "But quitting won't fix it." She explained that Kim was willing to talk things through. "I'll help you say what needs to be said—but you need to hear her too."

Ashley hesitated, then nodded.

Back in the conference room, Jo proposed a reset. "Let's meet tomorrow—neutral ground, fresh start." They decided on a coffee shop after Kim's school drop-off.

That night, Jo reflected. If they wanted to move forward, each of them would have work to do.

Being Vigilant and Supporting Others

We addressed in the previous chapter the many roles we can play to help others through mediation. Identifying these roles and understanding how mediation can apply in each context will prepare you to step in and assist when the need arises—and when that need is great.

Jo did not expect to mediate a workplace conflict, much less one involving her boss! In the chaotic buses we board, presumptive leaders falter, and unassuming passengers step up. Jo demonstrated leadership in that moment. She also demonstrated calm, patience, and a quiet approach so that Kim and Ashley could process their concerns with her before they all met. She did not excuse unhelpful behaviors, nor did she judge them. She saw the humanness in each and encouraged them to see the same in the other. She did this without betraying confidences and trusted the process to allow matters to unfold as needed.

Yet Jo's "in the moment" response was less spontaneous than may first appear. Kim and Ashley's willingness to accept her help was based on the trusting relationship she had already established. Jo had every reason to be as upset as Ashley. She'd lost status and did not perceive Kim as an effective leader. She understood the need for patience and for trusting in the process of change as the result of unanticipated and tragic circumstances.

Spectrum of Needs

Like Michelle in that bus ride, we, as everyday mediators, must offer grace and respite to those in need of our support with a call equivalent to "you can sit here." What is this call and when would it be useful? There is no one-size-fits-all, but the immediacy of our call depends on the immediacy of the need. Let's observe these needs and associated call-outs along a spectrum.

Evolving Need: "I Wonder"

Sometimes, a subtle concern catches your attention—a coworker hesitating before approaching someone, a child withdrawing from a friend, or an employee skirting around a deeper issue. The situation isn't urgent, but you sense that something is off. At this stage, surfacing concerns without jumping into action is key. The person may handle it alone but could benefit from talking it through. Try opening the conversation with gentle curiosity:

- "I wonder if something more is going on. Are you and Jake getting along okay?"
- "I wonder if there is something you're not saying. Is there something else you'd like me to know? I'm listening."
- "You haven't had a problem working with John before. It makes me wonder—what's going on?"

Using "I wonder" helps show concern without judgment, creating space for the other person to share—or choose not to share—on their own terms.

Evolved Need: "I Notice"

When a conflict becomes more apparent—lingering tension, stalled progress, or ongoing avoidance—it may be time to step in. The issue hasn't exploded, but a little guidance could prevent escalation. Your intervention could help because one or both individuals lack the essential courage, skills, or awareness of the need. You have moved from "I wonder" to "I notice." The prefatory "I notice" is helpful but not required in every situation:

- "I've noticed that you two aren't talking like you used to. Can I help?"
- "You mentioned before your concerns about working with Sam on this project, and you said you had it under control. But I've noticed more tension lately, and the project isn't moving forward. Perhaps I can help you two talk it through?"
- "I'm seeing real sadness when you mention Jane and how you don't play together anymore. Maybe there's something we can do so you can be friends again."

Urgent Need: "Please Take a Seat!"

Some conflicts demand immediate action: open hostility, repeated negativity, or full-blown arguments. Though others may tolerate the dysfunction, you recognize the need to step in. Perhaps your gentler "I notice" has fallen on deaf ears, but one or both individuals have clearly not demonstrated any ability or willingness to work things out. It is time to tell the individuals, in essence, to "sit down—now!" (At least that is the underlying message, though you may choose other words and a different tone depending on the urgency of the situation.) Depending on the urgency, your approach may vary:

- Repeated complaints: "Maggie, I've heard your remarks about Steve for a while now. This isn't

helping you or the team. Let's sit down with him and work this out."
- A heated exchange: "Whoa, let's slow down! We're not going to solve this by arguing. Let's talk."
- A full-out blowup: "Stop! That's enough. Take a seat."

Your response depends on your role, relationship, and awareness of the situation. Though many would opt out, stepping in with a mediator's mindset can make a real difference. Instead of avoiding the fire, run toward it—your instincts will guide you. Your role will depend on multiple factors, including how close you are to the individuals, your relationship with them (boss, friend, coworker, etc.), how aware you are about the situation, how long the matter has been going on, and how intense the matter is. You can opt out. Or you can remember that you have the capacity to help. Your "in the moment" instincts will guide you to decide how, when, and in what capacity to offer support.

Suggest a Different Approach

Those less familiar with the concept of third-party help or those who don't know you well may require further explanation about the following:

- **How you'll help.**

    - **Possible response:** "I'm just suggesting that we sit down and perhaps I can help you talk through concerns. You can decide how you'll proceed or whether a solution is possible. I simply want to help ensure that you are talking and listening to one another."

- **How the process will help them.**

    - **Possible response:** "You both seem so frustrated with the situation and what you've done so far (avoiding, arguing, taking positions, blaming, etc.) isn't working. Perhaps I can help you work past these obstacles. Sometimes a third party (or friend, colleague, HR representative, etc.) can help smooth things out a little so you can get down to what is truly troubling you."

- **What to expect.**

    - **Possible response:** "If you'll allow me, I'll make sure you each have a chance to talk through your concerns in a way that you feel heard. We may need a few ground rules such as 'no interruptions' and 'listen before you speak.' We'll spend time hearing one another out and then seeing where you disagree and whether we can find common ground. You can decide if it's helpful and an agreement is possible."

- **What might be achieved.**

    - **Possible response:** "Who knows what we might accomplish? You might improve your relationship (or complete the project on time, become friends again, improve communication, understand each other's viewpoint better, etc.) Surely, we can at least begin to understand where you are each coming from and, if we are successful, find a way to move forward."

These are general examples for gently persuading others of the value of mediation. Consider other messaging and "talking points" to make your case, depending on circumstances. Also note the absence of "mediator," "mediation," and similar words that may suggest more formality than others would expect, even though mediation is what you are offering. Consider the level of formality that's needed and resonates. Institutional representatives, such as HR representatives, may call it "mediation" because that is the service they routinely offer. Friends helping friends involves less formality where the term "mediation" may come across as odd.

Expect and Address Resistance

People in conflict become naturally apprehensive about sitting down together. They may think, "It hasn't worked before. Why should your proposal be any different?" As such, you'll need to anticipate possible resistance points and suggest counterpoints to consider in order to respond in the moment. Here are some common concerns regarding resistance:

- **One or both individuals believe there is nothing to mediate.**

    - **Possible response:** "The fact that you aren't talking to one another (or are arguing all the time, attacking each other, etc.) suggests that there are issues you both need to address. I know you feel it's all on him, but that is rarely the case. There is likely something you are doing, or that you could do differently, that Jack would appreciate, and that might help you work better with him."

- **They can't move beyond personal concerns they have about the other person.**

  - **Possible response:** "I know you feel that resolution isn't possible. Rachel seems impossible to work with, and it's futile to try. What's different this time is that I'll be there to help you communicate. Perhaps I can help ensure that Rachel really hears your concerns. You won't have to face her alone."

- **They doubt their ability to engage in the process.**

  - **Possible response:** "Whenever you or Rachel gets upset or doesn't know what to say next, I can help keep you on track. Believe me: I want you both to be able to communicate your concerns and feel as comfortable as possible. I think you're more capable than you realize in sharing your concerns and getting your point across. I will help you say what needs to be said."

- **They doubt your ability to help them.**

  - **Possible response:** "I'm not a miracle worker. I simply believe that we can work things out if we can sit down and talk things through. I'd like to think that I've demonstrated my concern and willingness to help—and at least some ability to help you communicate. If it doesn't work, I'll be the first to admit it and help find some other solution. Or perhaps someone else can help you talk through your concerns."

- **They doubt that the process will be effective.**

    ◦ **Possible response:** "There are no guarantees, but you might be surprised. It's worth a shot before dismissing it out of hand. Surely, that's better than continuing as you have."

- **They doubt that the process will be fair.**

    ◦ **Possible response:** "I'm not taking sides here. But I can help you be fully heard and encourage you to consider possibilities that will work for both of you. If you feel that the process isn't working, then say so. If I'm not facilitating conversation in a fair manner, say so. We'll talk it through and keep working it out until we reach an outcome that you both can agree to."

There is no cookie-cutter language, and these examples do not contemplate every scenario. Addressing resistance requires anticipating an individual's reservations and considering how you will respond. If you were in the person's shoes, what reservations would you have? Is it the process, the other person, or your involvement? What would you want to hear in order to feel more assured, calm, and hopeful during the bumpy ride?

Get People to the Table (or the Coffee Shop)

If you've persuaded individuals of the value of mediation, your next task is to find a time and place to meet. Here are some initial considerations:

- **Where will you meet?**

    Ideally, the space offers privacy, meaning it is removed from places where the participants engage in daily work and where prying eyes and ears may be present. Though this may just be a conference room in an office setting, readily accessible, convenient office spaces aren't realistic in many everyday conflict situations. Buses and planes aren't inherently private or formal, but it's where conflicts occur and require immediate attention. We can't always wait for the niceties of business life.

    As for privacy, which is always important, privacy from whom and what? Friends helping friends may find themselves mediating in a loud coffee shop while disinterested patrons sip special blends and tap at laptops oblivious to the turmoil. I am not suggesting we shun soundproof, closed-door spaces but that we be creative, use sound judgment, and let form fit function. Think of the following:

    - Can two colleagues go for coffee or find a park bench in the shade on a pleasant spring day?
    - Can friends mediate while walking along a nature trail?
    - Can a college student bring her two closest friends into her bedroom and have them sit on the bed or cross-legged on the floor?
    - Can business professionals meet in the hotel lobby amid the bustle of a conference?
    - Instead of a table, could neighbors use lounge chairs, floor mats, tree houses, sandy beaches, or other places where the accoutrements of formal business are absent?

The answer to all of these questions is a resounding "yes!"

- **What about meeting online?**

    This has become the go-to method for all sorts of meetings, and mediation is no exception. However, there are limitations. Even with cameras on, the virtual space can't account for the immediacy, intimacy, and interpretation of nonverbal messages that occur more fluidly face-to-face. Though it may seem more private, concerns about recording, having an unexpected guest (besides the cat!) listening in the wings, and other compromises to confidentially may present greater challenges than meeting in person does. These matters simply require adaptation to the unique dynamics of online interactions.

- **When will you meet?**

    Immediacy, particularly for conflicts that have erupted, suggests that NOW is the time to meet. Circumstances will guide your judgment. You may have addressed immediate concerns when you initiated a conversation "in the moment" to get individuals thinking about mediation and why meeting soon is important. Some situations may require a cooling-off period. Immediacy means considering the best and earliest time when the participants are better able to focus than at present.

- **How long will you meet?**

    As you address the timing, consider how long you'll need. Though you may think you'll need more time because it seems impossible to meaningfully address all the issues involved in a more compressed timeframe, meeting for long periods over emotional issues can be draining. On the other hand, you need sufficient time to discuss matters without feeling rushed. Consider these parameters:

    - Ninety minutes to two hours is the ballpark timeframe to determine whether resolution is possible. This timeframe also allows for participants to become a little tired and naturally let go of some of their resistance. (Tip: Ask for their whole morning or afternoon, or roughly three hours in case you are making progress and want to continue. You also don't want them to feel pressured about having to rush off to some other commitment.)
    - If more time is needed, schedule it soon—within a couple days to no more than a week.
    - Add a half hour or so if you meet online because you may need to slow down the process of listening and ensure that participants feel fully understood, which occurs a little less naturally in virtual environments. Breaks are needed for any mediation, but a little more time may be needed as a respite from so-called "Zoom fatigue."

These parameters, of course, are just that: parameters. College students meeting in the mediator's dorm room may meet for 15 minutes, then a half hour later in the cafeteria, and then later that night after studying. Further, for quickly evolving, can't-wait situations, timeframes are irrelevant. The mediation will take as long as it takes and end when it ends. It may take one short meeting, all afternoon, or multiple meetings in random places and during random times.

Use a Different Approach if the Table Isn't Set (or the Coffee Isn't Ready)

People in conflict are not always prepared to sit next to or across from their perceived adversary in order to talk through their differences. Others may welcome your advice but not your participation in mediation, feeling that they must confront the other person on their own, eventually. There are alternative approaches for assisting others with their conflicts when mediation isn't currently viable. Consider the following:

- **Shuttle diplomacy.** Shuttle diplomacy, often used in international negotiations and legal mediations, involves intermediaries communicating between parties to negotiate agreements. It requires trust in the process, as the mediator conveys only agreed-upon information, balancing persuasion with neutrality to encourage direct engagement.
- **Coaching others through conflict.** Conflict coaching helps individuals address disputes by analyzing the situation, communication dynamics, and potential solutions. Unlike mediation, coaching empowers individuals to navigate conflicts themselves, with options ranging from monitoring the situation to seeking third-party assistance or formal resolutions.[3]
- **Process advocacy.** Process advocacy ensures fair and objective handling of concerns, often seen in ombuds roles and also in everyday support efforts.[4] It involves guiding individuals toward appropriate

resources, facilitating communication with decision-makers, and advocating for fair procedures rather than specific outcomes.
- **Counseling.** Though mediation may lead to personal insights, unresolved emotional struggles may require professional counseling. Recognizing when mediation is no longer beneficial and referring individuals to appropriate support services ensures their well-being while maintaining the integrity of the mediation process.

Mediation often begins in the moments we least expect—when a passing comment, a tense interaction, or an unspoken hesitation signals an opportunity to step in. By staying vigilant, you can recognize when support is needed and how to guide individuals toward a constructive conversation. Whether through subtle curiosity ("I wonder"), direct acknowledgment ("I notice"), or firm intervention ("Take a seat"), your ability to respond in the moment sets the stage for resolution.

However, not everyone welcomes mediation right away. Resistance—whether due to fear, pride, or skepticism—is natural. By understanding these dynamics, you can approach hesitant participants with patience and flexibility, adapting your response to their readiness.

Recognizing the moment is only the beginning. The next practice is offering a seat—creating the space and structure for a productive dialogue. In the next chapter, we'll explore how to prepare participants for mediation, ensuring that they feel heard, safe, and ready to engage.

Chapter 3 Reflective Exercise

Prepare to "Respond in the Moment"

Use this reflection activity when a conflict situation is evolving, has evolved, or is urgent for which you can serve as mediator. Consider the information provided in this chapter and the question prompts to prepare yourself as you encourage others to engage in mediation.

Please note: situations requiring immediate attention may not allow you to engage in the note-taking and pre-planning that this exercise suggests. Instead, use the question prompts to reflect on how, in retrospect, you might have handled the situation. Post-reflection will benefit you for future encounters.

Every situation is different, so adapt this tool as best meets your needs. For an example, see the resources section at the end of this book.

My Mediation—Notes for "Responding in the Moment"
Participants:

-
-

(add additional participants as needed)

General notes on the conflict situation:

- How immediate is the need to respond? Determine the urgency, then jot down the kind of statements and messages you might share to respond at the appropriate moment. Refer back to the first section on the "Spectrum of Needs" for further insight. If you have already dealt with the situation, reflect on what you did and what you might do differently in the future.

- ○ Evolving need ("I wonder…" or similar messages and statements)
- ○ Evolved need ("I notice…" or similar messages and statements)
- ○ Urgent need ("Please take a seat" or similar messages and statements)

- Participant A:

- Participant B:

- How will you suggest mediation or a mediation-type communication process? Look back at "Suggest a Different Approach" and consider the "talking points" you'll use to encourage the individuals to sit down and engage in the appropriate conversation.

- Participant A:

- Participant B:

- What resistance do you anticipate? Look back at "Expect and Address Resistance" and jot down the specific kinds of resistance that each individual might offer, such as concerns about the effectiveness of the process, lack of trust in the other person, your ability to assist, etc. and how you might respond.

Second Practice: Respond in the Moment

- <u>Participant A:</u>

- <u>Participant B:</u>

- What preliminary plan might you suggest for getting them to the table? Where? When? For how long? Look back at "Get People to the Table (or the Coffee Shop)" and take note of issues, concerns, and logistical considerations for arranging the appropriate time, place, and space.

    - Where?

    - When?

    - For how long?

    - Other logistical considerations:

Chapter 4

Third Practice: Offer a Seat

Provide a Safe Place to Meet

"You can sit here."

Chapter Goals

By the end of this chapter, you will:

- be prepared to effectively prepare participants for mediation,

- understand how to build trust and create a safe environment using appropriate procedures, and

- appreciate how to initiate the mediation process with appropriate introductory remarks.

Conflict often feels unsafe. People in conflict may acknowledge the need to work through concerns, or they may resist the idea out of fear and perceived threats. They risk being vulnerable, exposed, embarrassed, called to account, or any number of other dreaded outcomes if they let go of their resistance. They also might resist because they don't trust the person or people with whom they are in conflict or may not trust you to help as mediator.

We must establish trust and demonstrate that we care and will treat their issues like we would our own baby. We must handle matters confidentially and ensure that we will not take sides or, put another way, that we will take both (or all) sides to ensure that they each are able to advocate for their interests, listen fully, understand the other's concerns, and feel fully heard.

In the previous chapter, we addressed skills and tools for encouraging people to engage in mediation. Maybe you've established the place and time to meet. You found the bus seat but must now make it a place for talking and listening safely amid the chaos. Participants may still have questions and even some doubts. You must make additional effort to establish safety and trust in the process—and in yourself as mediator.

A Story: "Offer a Seat" in Action

Max, an employee-relations specialist in HR, was asked to mediate a conflict between Tamara, a training manager, and Audrey, the newest trainer on Tamara's team, who were struggling with communication. In separate meetings, Audrey expressed frustration with Tamara's micromanaging, feeling she lacked the freedom given to other trainers. She spoke openly, often sharing tangential details. Tamara, more reserved and measured, appreciated Audrey's engaging style but felt she lacked polish and preparation. Despite coaching attempts, communication remained difficult.

When they met for mediation, Max suggested a few norms, such as to listen first before responding and not to interrupt when the other is talking. Before he could ask whether either participant had norms they wanted to suggest, Audrey jumped in.

"Can I ask a question? What if someone doesn't speak up? What if they just sit there and don't say anything, especially when they know they should? Isn't that a problem as well?"

Third Practice: Offer a Seat

"Is there a norm you want to suggest?" Max inquired.

"I don't know. I get that we shouldn't interrupt each other, but I think it's more likely for Tamara not to speak up when she should, or when she's bothered about something I'm saying. I'd like to know what she's thinking, but I can never tell. It can be frustrating."

Max took a moment to let these comments sink in.

"Well," he replied, "We won't know how Tamara will respond until we start talking, but obviously this concern is important to you. So let's give Tamara a chance to respond."

Tamara sat passively, looking down at the table, clearly tense and uncomfortable.

"See, that's what I'm talking about," proclaimed Audrey. "I can't know what she's thinking. Then, after I've done something, she asks to meet and tells me all the things I've done wrong. I'm afraid she's going to sit here now, let me do all the talking, then pounce later."

"Let's hold up," said Max. "We can give this time. Tamara, when you're ready."

"I don't mind responding," Tamara replied after a moment. "I've come to realize that Audrey needs time to vent, and I try to allow her to do that. Then, that is perceived as passive. When I do say something to help Audrey in her job, she can't focus. She doesn't want to hear it."

"That's not true," countered Audrey. "I listen. But too many times, you let me go off and do my work and then criticize later."

"How can I offer input? I don't *let* you go off to work; you simply run off without hearing me."

"And when you do give input, it seems so unfair. You don't treat others this way."

"Well, that's why we're here, isn't it?" Tamara remarked, looking at Max.

Max took a moment. Then he asked Tamara, "So you've heard Audrey's concern. You have concerns of your own. How would you express them as a norm for us to consider today?"

"I'm content with what you've already suggested," she responded. "I'll listen. I'll try to reflect on what Audrey says before I respond. I hope Audrey can do the same."

Audrey reacted to this, which led to another tense exchange. But at least they were talking, thought Max.

"Well," he said eventually, "Let me try to sum up what I think are important norms for each of you, and you can tell me if they work for you. Audrey, you want to ensure that Tamara tries fully to understand what you've said and acknowledges it, and doesn't simply passively take it in. You don't want there to be a vacuum where Tamara isn't responding. Is that the general idea?"

Audrey responded, "Yes, I guess that's it," but looked as if she wanted to say more.

"If there is a different way you would express it, let's understand that."

"No, I think we're good."

"You can also call attention to your concern without waiting for me. Simply note when you'd like a response from Tamara and we can ask her. Will that work?"

"Yes, that should work. Thank you."

"And Tamara, you want to be sure that when you do respond, Audrey listens and doesn't become reactive, either talking over you and disagreeing before you've had a chance to finish or shutting down and, well, changing the subject. You'd like her to slow down and consider carefully what you've said—to give the same consideration you give her. Does that cover it?"

"Yes, I think so," replied Tamara.

"Okay," Max asserted, "I think I've got it. And I'll do my part to help you each follow through on what we've discussed. Can you each agree to these norms we've discussed today?"

Both agreed. Max completed introductory remarks and asked who would like to begin.

Prepare the Participants
From this story, you can see how Max helped to prepare the participants about what comes next. The actual mediation hadn't even started yet, but a lot was accomplished. He gathered insights into each participant's concerns, communication styles, and frustrations, allowing him to anticipate potential challenges during mediation. By giving Audrey and Tamara space to express their perspectives separately, he helped them feel heard and validated, setting a foundation for a more constructive dialogue. Additionally, he established initial ground rules and began to address underlying tensions, ensuring that both participants understood the importance of open and honest communication. This preparation stage not only set expectations but also built trust in the mediation process, increasing the likelihood of a productive conversation.

From Max's action and dialogue, we see the following process unfold:

1. **Reinforce the process.** Reiterate the mediation process to ensure that participants understand what to expect. This builds confidence and reduces uncertainty.
2. **Provide a safe forum.** Some participants may be hesitant or fearful. Creating a space for them to express concerns before the mediation helps ease anxiety.
3. **Gather perspectives.** Obtain a general understanding of each participant's viewpoint in order to anticipate key issues and resistance points. This is often their first chance to articulate their concerns without judgment.

4. Address concerns. Discuss any potential issues regarding the participants' behavior, clarify your role as mediator, and ensure that they feel heard and protected in the process.

5. Encourage outcome planning. Guide participants to think about their ideal resolution, tangible goals, and potential walk-away points—without coaching or directing their decisions.

6. Foster trust. Reinforce confidentiality, encourage questions, and affirm their commitment to the process, being sure to maintain a calm and supportive presence.

Holding Separate Pre-Mediation Meetings

Max met separately with Tamara and Audrey before they all met together. This is a common practice but one to approach carefully in order to maintain neutrality and avoid bias during mediation. Some mediators choose not to engage in them for that reason. Friends mediating for friends may find them unnecessary. Depending on your comfort level with ambiguity, you may decide to hold brief separate meetings when you are less familiar with the participants or the situation. There are three purposes for holding separate meetings:

1. **To understand the situation.** This is not an interrogation or an investigation. You don't need to know every detail, just enough to get a general sense of what's going on and each participant's unique perspective. The full story will unfold as it needs to during mediation.

2. **To explain the process.** You will do this anyway as you start the mediation, but it may be helpful for participants to understand what to expect beforehand. Generally, you will cover the same information as provided in this chapter regarding introductory statements.

3. To provide general guidance. Participants may have questions about how to approach the mediation and/or the other participant. You might ask them to consider their goals, negotiation strategy, or bottom-line (or walk-away) considerations or provide general suggestions for how to conduct themselves. Use your judgment for what you suggest, but be careful not to cross a line and act like their advisor or coach. Have them think for themselves; don't do their thinking for them.

Establish a Physical Space That Is Safe and Supportive

When we talk about a safe space, we are not necessarily talking about physicality. In the previous story, a safe space meant a feeling of being heard in a way they each needed, and it was something Max could offer when he went off-script. It took insight, creativity, and judgment to put aside a rendition of a script to mediate in the moment.

Max spent time with Audrey to understand her concerns about Tamara's tendency to take everything in, not respond, and then pounce later. Tamara agreed to be more cognizant of the issue during mediation. Max would also help whenever Audrey expressed a concern. Tamera expressed her own concerns about Audrey's tendency to deflect without listening. She needed to feel that Audrey would take her comments seriously and not "run off." Max would need to ensure that Audrey was taking time to listen and reflect on what Tamara was saying.

It was clear to Max that the overriding issue was how each communicated and would fail to pick up on the other's cues. It led to two norms, one each proposed by Tamara and Audrey, that would go a long way in addressing their challenges as long as Max could simply hold them to these norms. He could then ensure that they could each raise their respective concerns when needed and take time to work through each matter before moving forward.

Set the Stage Informally for Informal Mediated Settings
For more formal mediations or where possible in everyday mediations, the process should occur in a private, neutral, and comfortable space that encourages open dialogue. Whereas the previous chapter covered logistics such as time and location, here we focus on how the environment shapes communication, decision-making, and reconciliation. Key considerations include the following:

- **Neutrality.** Avoid hosting mediation in a participant's office or home, as doing so could create power imbalances. The space should be welcoming for all but not overly cozy or distracting.
- **Comfort without distraction.** Provide basic essentials—notepads, pencils, tissues, and water—while avoiding harsh lighting, extreme temperatures, or clutter. Seating should be comfortable and not too rigid or soft.
- **Seating arrangements.** A round table minimizes "side-taking," whereas a rectangular table should be positioned to encourage collaboration rather than opposition. Seating side by side can shift the mindset from adversarial to problem-solving in partnership.
- **Safety and accessibility.** Consider ease of entry and exit, proximity to restrooms, and accommodations for all participants. If necessary, provide a second room for private conversations.

For virtual mediations, ensure a professional background, good lighting, and clear audio. Encourage participants to keep cameras on and minimize distractions, while allowing for short breaks when needed.

The right space fosters trust and engagement. Though an ideal setup is helpful, adaptability is key—work with what you have and focus on the mediation itself.

Begin Mediation with Welcoming, Supportive Introductory Remarks

If you have prepared the participants well and provided a safe space, your next step should be relatively easy. This involves introductory remarks appropriate to the situation. Max's meeting with Audrey and Tamara occurred in a pre-arranged business setting, so he likely prepared a brief, structured introductory statement. Other settings are less formal and call for more impromptu, but no less thoughtful, introductory remarks.

Consider an Introductory Script for More Formal Settings

Mediators routinely begin with prepared remarks to explain the process and their role, set communication norms, and create a supportive environment for communication and decision-making. They also address issues such as confidentiality, neutrality, potential conflicts of interests, and other matters appropriate for the mediation or as required within their field of practice.[5] A sample introductory statement suitable for everyday mediation is provided in the resources section. The best practice is to prepare your introductory statement beforehand. The script is a baseline. Don't repeat it verbatim. Capture the main points you want to stress as bullets and put them in your own words. The reflective exercise for this chapter provides additional guidance and question prompts for doing this.

Use Your Intuition to Make the Introductory Remarks Needed for the Situation

In everyday mediation, you'll likely be with friends or colleagues who trust you. And if so, they will trust you to facilitate a conversation that supports them both, so specific references to confidentiality, neutrality, and impartiality may be omitted from your script or informal remarks. These informal interactions will also omit discussion of legal and policy considerations, which is the purview of mediators in more formal settings. Such matters simply wouldn't occur to you as you try to help them talk through matters in a more civilized manner. Your "in the moment" introductory remarks might, therefore, be as simple as one of the following:

- "Let's sit down and talk about this. I think we need to clear the air or there won't be any point in talking about plans for a vacation."
- "I think it's time we work this thing out. You've been at this far too long and seem to be talking past one another. Come on. Let's get a cup of coffee and talk about it. I'll buy."
- "You know, it hurts to see you two go at it like this. This isn't like you. What's going on? Let's sit down and talk about it. Something's bothering you both, and I want to help straighten it out so we can get back to the way things were."

If, in contrast to these examples, you have time to plan, such as agreeing to meet the next day for coffee, your introductory remarks still shouldn't be too elaborate. You might begin this way:

> "Thanks for meeting today. I'm really glad we could sit down to talk about this situation. I know it

Third Practice: Offer a Seat

hasn't been easy for you. And thanks for allowing me to try to help you. I'll go ahead and get some coffee, and when I come back, we'll see what we can accomplish to talk about this issue and try to find a way to move forward. Candice, how do you like your coffee? Rob, what about you?"

[After idle chitchat where you share common ground about your love of dogs, leading to some laughter] "They're a member of the family, just like our kids—and better behaved! It's great to have a good laugh about it. Thanks, again, for meeting with me this morning. I hope we can have a productive conversation about what happened yesterday. And really, I hope we can just take a breath and relax about it. We can figure this out. Now that we've had some time to sleep on it, maybe we can find a way to resolve your concerns. That's my hope, anyway."

These examples don't suggest a lot of ground rules which may not be necessary, depending on the relationships involved and the trust they've placed in you. You might simply transition from your beginning statement to a statement like, "Brian, let's have you go first, if that's okay," or a question such as, "Who would like to start?" If it is important to establish some general expectations for communicating, keep it informal. Consider these examples:

- "Why don't we proceed this way? Blair, perhaps you could begin since you raised the concern initially. And Una, let me encourage you to listen to what Blair has to say. Let's be sure we understand what Blair

is saying, then we'll give you the same chance. That sound okay to you?"
- "If we want things to be different this time, let's make an effort to listen to one another. I'll help you. But I want to encourage you to hear what the other person is saying without interrupting, reflect on what you've heard, and then, once he feels heard, we'll reverse the process so you have the same opportunity."
- [After first discussing basic listening expectations] "One other thing I've noticed: I know it's frustrating, but we can show our frustration with our face, such as rolling our eyes, and with our voice, like heavy sighs and grunts and groans. Let's watch that. Try not to be reactive to what you're hearing. You'll get your chance to respond."
- [As a participant begins early to interrupt] "Jack, this is what I've been talking about—and I think has been bothering Toni. It's this constant need to get a word in. We need to watch that. Unless we can each share openly without being interrupted and feel that we'll be talked over before we can get a word in edgewise, we won't get anywhere. Do you think you can do that?"

Even as you start, you may be challenged. Who appointed you savior? What makes you special? Why should they trust you? Whose side are you on anyway? And so forth. Based on the context, respond in the appropriate manner to address the concern:

- "Look, I'm frustrated too, and as far as I can see, so is the team. They want to see you get through this. If you don't want my help, say so. I just think it's about time we get a handle on this."

- "I've got to be honest. I've been caught between the two of you for too long. You can't keep coming to me, complaining about each other. If you trust me to complain to me, you'll trust me to complain together. Here. Now. In the same room. Together."
- "I'm just concerned about you. Isn't that enough? I don't want to see you walk away from a good thing. And that's what you have, isn't it? So let me try to help, if you're both willing."
- "Oh, no, we've been best friends too long to let things fall apart over something so petty. We're going to work this thing out if it kills us."
- "This is just between the three of us. No one else needs to know. I'm certainly not going to tell anyone."

Additional Considerations

Effective mediation goes beyond following a script—it requires adaptability, awareness, and the ability to create a safe, open space for discussion. Whether in a formal setting or an impromptu conversation, mediators must foster collaboration, adjust their approach based on the situation, and maintain confidence in their ability to guide the process. The following principles outline key strategies for successful mediation, helping ensure that all participants feel heard, respected, and empowered to work toward a resolution.

1. Use inclusive language. Saying "we" instead of "you" fosters a sense of shared responsibility and avoids singling out individuals. This approach reduces defensiveness, normalizes common challenges, and reinforces that everyone—including the mediator—is working toward resolution together. It sets a collaborative tone, making it easier for participants to engage openly.

2. Adapt to context. Every mediation situation is different. Some may require a direct approach, whereas others need a softer touch. Consider the personalities involved, the nature of the conflict, and the setting. In more formal settings, professionalism is key, whereas in casual or workplace conflicts, a conversational approach may work better. Let your intuition guide your tone and communication style to ensure that your message is well received.

3. Be confident. Mediation is about reading the room and responding in a way that feels natural and effective. Though structured guidance can help, it's important to trust your instincts, stay flexible, and be yourself. Confidence reassures participants that you can guide them through the process, even in challenging situations. Approach mediation as a supportive peer rather than an authoritative figure.

4. Ensure safety anywhere. Not all mediations happen in ideal conditions. Conflicts can arise in coffee shops, in conference lobbies, or even during casual outings. Though a private setting is best, it's not always an option. Learn to create a sense of safety wherever you are by adjusting seating arrangements, lowering voices, or suggesting a brief walk to a quieter space. Your ability to maintain a calm, neutral presence helps establish trust, even in less-than-ideal environments.

By applying the principles outlined in this chapter, you will be well equipped to guide participants through the mediation process with confidence and clarity. Effective preparation helps set the stage for constructive dialogue, ensuring that all parties feel heard and understood. By building trust and establishing a safe environment, you create the conditions necessary for open communication and meaningful resolution.

Initiating mediation with clear, structured statements reinforces your neutrality and provides participants with a framework for productive discussions. Whether mediating formal disputes or facilitating everyday conflicts, your ability to set the tone, allow for collaboration, and adapt to different situations will determine the success of the process. As you continue developing your mediation skills, remember that every interaction is an opportunity to refine and build stronger relationships through thoughtful, inclusive communication.

Now that we've offered a seat, we can sit with them—the fourth practice along *The Mediation Road Map*.

Chapter 4 Reflective Exercise

Plan Your Introductory Remarks and Other Preliminary Details

Although a sample introductory statement is provided in the resources, please don't use it! More to the point, don't use a pre-written script at all. Instead, create a fresh statement or informal remarks for each mediation in order to ensure authenticity. This exercise will help you develop a natural, effective introduction.

Instructions:

1. **Identify key points.** List the essential topics you need to cover.
2. **Use the "introductory statement" tool:**
   - Review the question prompts for each item and write a few notes addressing key ideas.
   - Convert these notes into concise bullet points for delivery.
3. **Adapt as needed.** Some prompts may require more detail, others less. Adjust based on the situation and your comfort level. Use note-taking if needed.

Keep it natural—your genuineness matters more than perfection.

Introductory Statement
Participant A: _____
Participant B: _____
Date: _____

Welcome and introduction (How will you begin in order to show warmth and support for the participants and acknowledge their commitment to the process?):

-

Why we are here (How would you briefly describe the general nature of the conflict that has brought the participants to mediation?):

-

My role as mediator (What should you say to remind participants generally that you are there to support and facilitate the communication and leave decision-making to them?):

-

Overview and/or reminders of the general process for mediation (How will you describe in general terms what will happen today?):

-

Confidentiality, neutrality, and impartiality and what they mean (What are the general parameters you need to note as well as specific issues pertinent to the participants and their situation?):

-

Relevant disclosures, if any (What prior involvements, relationships with participants, or other potential conflicts do you need to disclose and discuss before proceeding? Don't forget to get their assent for you to continue as mediator.):

-

Norms for talking (What norms and ground rules are important for this situation? Will you suggest them, have the participants suggest them, or both suggest and have participants suggest them?):

-

Separate meetings and their purpose (How will you describe what occurs in separate meetings, when they may be needed, and how they may be utilized?):

-

Third Practice: Offer a Seat

Reaffirmations before beginning (What further words of encouragement do you need to share in order to show appreciation, positive regard, and hope in participants' ability to achieve resolution?):

-

Additional considerations (What additional comments do you need to share and discuss?):

- Notetaking
    -
- Consultation with third parties
    -
- Legal and policy parameters
    -
- Inclusion of nonessential others
    -
- Other logistical considerations (bathrooms, vending, parking vouchers, etc.)
    -

Other issues or concerns (What other matters not previously covered do you need to address before beginning the mediation?):

-

Chapter 5

Fourth Practice: Sit with Others

Create Environments for Talking, Listening, and Empathy Amid the Chaos

"We are safe here. You can talk. I will listen."

Chapter Goals

By the end of this chapter, you will:

- embrace facilitating open and supportive communication processes,
- deepen your empathic listening and encourage participants to do the same, and
- be equipped to capture stories and perspectives for consideration later.

People in conflict have stories to tell. Some stories are short and succinct. Others, particularly when difficult emotions are involved, are long and given in nonlinear fashion. Facts matter, but they can also be obscured as a participant's story goes on, especially when nerves are involved and it's the first time the story has been told aloud, in full detail, in front of the person with whom there is a conflict. However, there is much to be discovered in the stories themselves that could help greatly with the mediation process.

Everyday mediators care about facts, of course, but we also provide time and space for storytelling by remaining present, sitting with the participants (literally and figuratively), and demonstrating empathy and deep listening. When we do this, we model the same for them so they may fully hear the other and feel fully heard themselves. They patiently work through the facts and emotions of divergent stories, uncover the bits and pieces that are most salient, and learn where differences and opportunities for common ground may lie to establish a beginning point for resolution.

Now that you've offered a safe place for talking, it's time to sit with the participants so they can share their experiences, concerns, and perspectives about their conflict.

A Story: "Sit with Others" in Action

Allie, a calm and supportive PR professional, met with Cindy, director of PR and event planning, who asked her to mediate a conflict between Cindy's direct reports, Robert and Randi. Robert, an assistant director with 20 years of experience, valued traditional team collaboration, whereas Randi, a newer events manager, preferred efficiency and independent work. Their conflict centered on Robert's weekly meetings, which Randi found unproductive and overly social, whereas Robert felt that Randi dismissed team brainstorming and neglected the meetings.

From the start of the mediation, both seemed frustrated, and when Robert interrupted Randi, Allie remarked, "We discussed at the beginning how we would each give the other the chance to speak before responding. Let's listen to Randi, and you'll have your chance after that."

"Okay," Robert said, appearing dejected.

Randi continued, "Like I was saying, a lot of the meeting time is spent talking about their kids and the weekend, and it feels like if there is time for that, there should be time to discuss my ideas. So, over time, when meetings come up, if I have other business to tend to, I prioritize those issues because the meetings don't serve any useful purpose."

"So," reflected Allie, "you are concerned about how meetings are managed and how time is spent, which isn't respectful of your time and need for input. Is that the general idea?"

"Yes. It's just feeling that my ideas are never being heard."

"Thank you," said Allie. "I'm sure there may be other issues to discuss in a minute." Turning to Robert, "Robert, I know you want to respond."

"Yes."

"But before you do, could you put into your own words what you heard Randi say?"

"Well," responded Robert, "She doesn't like my meetings. She's just critical of them."

"Okay," said Allie, puzzled. "Is that what Randi said? Randi, is that what you said?"

"No," replied Randi. "The way the meetings are structured is my issue. So much of it is personal talk and not actually anything to drive our department forward."

"So there's some information around the issue of meetings that Randi is expressing. It's not just being critical. Could you try again, Robert? What did you hear Randi say?"

"Well, she's saying she doesn't like the way meetings are run. She feels like there's a lot of chitchat before any business is discussed. That's not true, but that's what I'm hearing her say."

"Thank you. Randi, do you feel that's a sufficient understanding of your concerns?"

"Yeah, that's fine."

Allie then encouraged Randi to further share her concerns and periodically asked Robert to reflect on her perspective. Though his responses weren't always accurate, Allie felt that they demonstrated a genuine attempt to understand Randi's viewpoint. After ensuring that Randi felt heard, she gave Robert the same opportunity.

Robert shared, "I've worked here over 20 years, and most of my team has too. We know each other well, and I prefer starting meetings by catching up. Randi claims I don't read her emails, but that's not true. She has good ideas, but we're more creative when we brainstorm together. She doesn't come to meetings, so I don't always respond. I think she doesn't respect how we collaborate."

Allie then gave Randi the chance to reflect, noticing she also expressed disagreement through nonverbal cues such as eye rolls, folded arms, and headshaking.

"Okay, thank you, Robert," said Allie. "I'm sure there are a few more issues to discuss. So, Randi, I want to ask that you do the same as what I asked Robert and reflect on what you heard. But could I make an observation for both of you? It may be something I should have checked regarding our norms, but let's watch how we're listening and look at our body language and think about that."

Robert looked confused, suggesting there was no problem with his body language.

"Actually, I'm referring to Randi as well," responded Allie. "I'd like us to consider how we are communicating and try to convey respectful messages as we listen to one another."

Allie paused a moment to allow her request to sink in. "Do you think you can do that?"

Randi and Robert nodded in agreement, and Allie encouraged Randi to reflect on Robert's statements. They alternated until Allie felt that enough information had been shared. Occasionally being prompted to speak directly, they did so imperfectly. Once mutual understanding was reached, Allie shifted focus to their differences and possible solutions. Despite lingering tension, her patience and guidance helped them move toward resolution.

Facilitate Open and Supportive Communication Processes

In this story, Allie allowed each participant to tell their story—not just the facts. What are the goals for storytelling? We are seeking to uncover, from each party's perspective, the facts of the situation and the emotions and interpretations underlying the facts. People take different routes to tell their stories. We can't force them to just "start from the beginning and go from there." We will tease out the story eventually, but they need the freedom to share in whatever fashion and at whatever point in time makes sense to them. Each person's story will unfold through listening, clarifying, telling, and retelling in response and juxtaposition to the other's story. We have to patiently allow each person's story to take shape over time.

Getting Started

To start, an everyday mediator might simply ask, "Who would like to begin?" to avoid implying that one person is more responsible for the conflict. If one participant initiated the mediation, say Juan, you might lead off with, "Juan, would you like to begin?" without emphasizing their role.

Depending on the relationship, one may naturally start or suggest that the other go first, with silent pauses being fine. If silence persists, you can say, "We can wait. There's no rush—whenever you're ready." It doesn't matter who speaks first.

If they remain hesitant or only gripe without telling their story, return to expectations and norms for talking. Be patient—some mediations take longer to get started than others do.

Facts vs. Emotions

Facts may seem straightforward, but differing emotions and interpretations make them complex. There's often no full agreement on what happened, why, and what it means.

Facts can be broken down into three types: *Who* facts relate to the participants or third parties involved, such as a couple or coworkers and their behaviors. *What* facts are tangible elements of the dispute, such as a boundary tree or assigned workload. *How* facts involve the details that have led to the conflict, such as communication styles between coworkers or attempts to address a shared issue.

Emotions and interpretations give these facts context, offering insights into why the conflict exists and persists.

Let's look at a few examples:

Who Frank and June, dispute in marriage	Frank's concern about June: She never wants to do what I want to do; she's so particular. June's concern about Frank: He's always busy and stressed; he never has time to go out.
Who Bill and George, coworkers	Bill's view of George: He works hard and is dedicated but doesn't take time to train me. George's view of Bill: He wants to do a good job but just doesn't get it.

Fourth Practice: Sit with Others

What Neighbor dispute regarding a tree	Maxine's interpretation of the situation: My tree is healthy and isn't going to fall on Pauline's house; I have insurance anyway, so what's the big deal? It gives Pauline's house shade. Pauline's interpretation: The tree is hollow and dead, and it's a matter of time before a storm will knock it down on my garage. I don't care about shade. I can't sell my house with that danger.
What Supervisor/ employee dispute about employee's workload	Supervisor's interpretation of the situation: We all have to chip in. Times are tough for everyone. Nasser just needs to suck it up. I can't trade off assignments to others; everyone is overloaded. He's not the hardest worker. Employee's interpretation: Michael is being unreasonable. There's too much to do, and it's unfair to always be under these pressures and then be poorly rated for not completing tasks that are impossible to complete in the timeframes expected.

How	
Dispute over communication styles, with concerns about bullying	Fiona's interpretation: It all started when Jasmine said I would just have to get used to her New York manner. It's harsh and offensive. It's simply an excuse for not giving a damn about what others think, especially me. Jasmine's interpretation: I would care about your views, Fiona, if you had any. Your quiet church-mouse style doesn't exactly instill confidence. I can't get you to react to anything I say or to offer your own suggestions.
How Neighbor dispute regarding a tree	Pauline's interpretation: I've tried to talk with Maxine about it. But anytime I suggest she do more to keep up her yard, she walks away. One time, she said, "You want to take care of my yard, feel free." She says she's always busy. She's a horrible neighbor, and that tree is an example. Maxine's interpretation: I am always busy, and I do the minimal necessary. I keep the yard mowed, and the tree takes care of itself. I keep it trimmed; otherwise, it's fine. What are you, the lawn-care police? Butt out!

Are we trying to get at "the truth"—that is, the absolute, objective truth as observed by a divine presence? No. We hope to understand truth as the participants understand it. We expect them to be truthful, but they are not bound by a witness oath. Mediation is not an evidentiary hearing, and many facts will remain unexplored as individuals home in on the facts, perspectives, and interpretations most important to them. Your challenge is to establish a coherent set of facts and an understanding about them that is sufficient to help the individuals move forward.

The Importance of Empathic Listening in Storytelling

The essential skill for uncovering the truth behind the conflict is listening—deep, profound listening.[6] Consider the following:

- *Are you a good listener?*
- *Do you sit up, square your shoulders, establish eye contact, and provide undivided attention?*
- *Do you interject short verbal cues of understanding such as "uh huh," "I see," and "I understand"?*
- *Do you nod your head, laugh when they laugh, sigh when they sigh, and show a concerned, caring expression when they share stories of pain and sorrow?*

If your answers are yes, you are demonstrating effective listening—but that is not enough. Though you provide appropriate cues to encourage the speaker to keep talking, these actions are only the mechanics of listening.

Even the most insincere "listeners" can do this. Consider the typical business meeting. Though conversation is polite, people remain entrenched in their positions and are no more inclined to concede another's point at the end of the meeting than when it began. They may say, "Please, let me understand your view," and then—recognizing that polite, genteel business etiquette demands some level of deference—shut up for a moment, only to take a breath and stop listening as they craft what they're going to say next to advance their unchanged, unexplored agenda.

    The essential and perhaps most powerful tool in the mediator's tool kit is the ability to demonstrate and listen with empathy. "Empathy" is defined as the capacity for "understanding, being aware of, being sensitive to, and vicariously experiencing the feelings, thoughts, and experiences of another."[7] The mediator is present during the bumpy ride as participants share their experiences. They don't need judges, critics, and scoffers. They need to feel that you can experience the difficulty or pain they feel as though you are sitting right next to them in real time as the experience is unfolding.

    A conversation imbued with empathy contrasts sharply with one involving only mechanics. When people say, "Please, let me understand your view," they mean it. We don't merely shut up in polite deference before unloading counterarguments. We allow time for others to share, sit with what we've heard, consider it, and attempt to demonstrate an understanding of what the person has communicated before formulating our response. These are the behaviors of an empathic listener. They include the following:

- **Paraphrasing:** "If I understand correctly, you are saying…"
- **Checking for agreement:** "Have I got that right? Is that what you are saying?"
- **Seeking clarification:** "I'm not sure I got that last point right. Tell me more about that. Are you saying *x* or are you saying *y*? Or am I off the mark completely?"
- **Finding agreement:** "It seems we are saying the same thing. You're saying *x* and I'm saying *y*, yet

it boils down to *z*. Wouldn't you agree or am I still missing something?"
- **Validating:** "You really tried to work things out with Joe. You tried to be fair."
- **Reflecting feelings:** "When you say Jerry ignores and dismisses your comments in meetings, you feel that he is condescending and disrespectful, and that angers you. Is that how you feel?"
- **Making empathetic statements** (e.g., single mother injured in a car accident): "Kimberly, I can only imagine what it was like to be in the car accident. I'm glad you're doing better. This experience must have been awful. You're now struggling with being off work due to your injury while taking care of three kids on your own. It must feel lonely and desperate. The stress must be overwhelming."

The last example takes a deep dive into empathy. It's an educated guess. You haven't lived Kimberly's hard-luck life and can only put yourself in her shoes to imagine her physical pain and long recovery—and how desperate and lonely it can be to raise children with no stable means of support. Anyone would feel overwhelmed. Yet what preceded your response may simply have been Kimberly's rendition of her life while fighting back tears and trying to remain professional in a mediation of her negligence case.

As you develop as a mediator, you will find the place to insert the appropriate level of empathy and utilize the appropriate listening skills to meet the participants' needs.

Check In to Ensure Understanding
Some examples end with check-ins such as "Is that what you're saying?" or "Is that how you feel?" These moments

are essential—they confirm understanding and invite clarification. By asking these questions, you signal that you are actively listening and genuinely interested in their perspective.

This process is powerful. When a participant corrects your interpretation, don't see it as a misstep; instead, view it as an opportunity to refine your understanding. Paraphrasing and reflecting back what you hear builds trust and helps uncover deeper concerns. Keep going back and forth until the person fully feels heard, not just acknowledged.

Even if they affirm your check-in, be cautious about accepting it too quickly. People often agree just to move the conversation along or to avoid conflict. If you sense hesitation, nonverbal cues such as a forced smile, a slight shrug, or an averted gaze may indicate that they're not entirely comfortable. In these moments, gently probe further: "Are you sure I understand? I want to be certain I've got this right."

This isn't just about achieving clarity—it's about demonstrating genuine care and respect. When people feel truly understood, they become more open to resolution and compromise. Aim for *full and complete understanding*, not just surface-level agreement. The difference between "Do you feel that I understand your position?" and "Do you feel that I fully and completely understand your perspective?" can be the key to fostering real connection and progress.

Model Empathic Listening
As a mediator, you guide participants back to natural communication and understanding. Good moments occur when you listen deeply to each participant; great moments occur when participants listen to each other. There is no more powerful tool for accomplishing this than empathic listening. It is pleasing to the mind, heart, and soul.

Fourth Practice: Sit with Others

In conflict, it takes courage to acknowledge shared responsibility. Someone must listen first, showing that the other person's perspective matters. By focusing on their concerns without interjecting, you set the stage for mutual understanding. Once you've fully listened, you can ask for the same in return, inviting questions to ensure clarity. You might ask, "May I now share my perspective and ask that you listen as I have done for you?" Encourage the person: "Please ask whatever questions you need because I really want to be sure you understand my perspective as I've tried to understand yours." Take breaks in your telling to encourage their inquiry, such as asking, "What questions do you have at this point?" or "What isn't clear to you?"

As a mediator, your role is to model empathic listening—not for yourself but to help participants do the same. You demonstrate that you are trying to understand each participant from their point of view. As you model with one, the other witnesses your actions, then you reverse this process to model with the other:

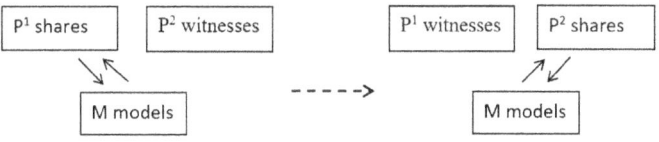

Modeling empathic listening sets the expectation that participants do the same. Ideally, they take over while you observe and support as needed.

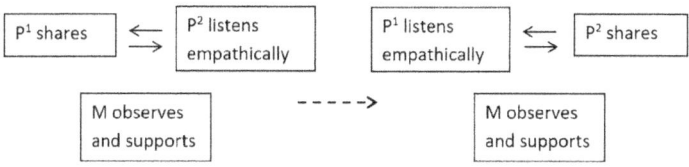

Modeling empathic listening is key, but getting participants to listen to each other matters more. Set expectations early: they must summarize the other's words before responding. This may slow the process, but it ensures that both feel heard. After one speaks, ask the other, "Before sharing your perspective, please state in your own words what you heard." Initially, responses may be dismissive:

Betty: "Fran is saying she doesn't like me."

Mediator: "Is that really what she said? Think about what she actually shared."

Betty (revising): "Fran feels that I don't listen and that I'm too critical, which frustrates her."

Mediator (to Fran): "Is that accurate?"

Fran: "Mostly, but I also love Betty—she's my best friend. Her criticism hurts, but I know she means well."

Mediator (to Betty): "Can you try again?"

Betty: "She doesn't like my criticism. She loves me."

Often, participants rush to defend themselves instead of truly listening:

Mediator: "Betty, what did you hear Fran say?"

Betty: "She says I'm harsh, but she never listens to my concerns, and she—"

Mediator (interrupting gently): "You'll have your turn. First, let's focus on what Fran is saying."

The mediator facilitates back-and-forth dialogue until both feel heard. Though conflicts are complex and time-consuming, reinforcing this process early makes it more natural. Some adapt quickly, whereas others need more guidance.

Use Additional Techniques for Encouraging Participant-to-Participant Listening

Ideally, participants make eye contact and use second-person language ("When you said that, I felt…"), but this often feels unnatural. Instead, they may look to you for safety, using third-person language ("What he did was…"). Be patient, especially when mistrust is high, but encourage direct communication when possible. Here are some ways to shift their focus to each other:

1. **Avoid eye contact.** Look down or toward the other participant instead. Without nonverbal cues from you, they may naturally start engaging directly.
2. **Use a hand gesture.** Extend your hand toward the person speaking and gently sweep it toward the other participant while breaking eye contact. If prepped in advance, they will recognize this cue.
3. **Prompt them directly.** Say, "You and I have been talking for a while, but could you speak directly to Kim now?" If needed, reinforce with, "Jerod, I know it's more comfortable talking to me, but it's important you address Kim directly."

Let Participants Tell Their Stories Their Way, Not Yours

Allowing participants to tell their stories in their own way is essential for building trust and genuine understanding. When people are given the space to express their experiences without interruption or imposed structure, they feel heard and validated. Forcing a specific narrative or steering their account to fit a predetermined framework can create resistance and deepen frustration. Instead, let them share in their own words, at their own pace, and in the order that feels most natural to them.

Clarifying vs. Probing

Traditional mediation processes often emphasize the search for facts as paramount to understanding the underlying emotions and interpretations that individuals place on facts. Mediators may not hesitate to ask probing questions—who, what, why, when, where, and how—throughout the course of the participants' narratives: "What happened then?" "Who were you talking to?" "How did you get there?" "When did that happen exactly?" "Why did you decide to...?" "Where were you at the time?"

Intense probing such as this can reflect arrogance. You appear to think that you know best which facts are important and don't trust the individual to state the right ones. Such questions create confusion and defensiveness because the storyteller finds themselves spending more time explaining and defending than naturally telling the story they need to tell.

Everyday mediation is different. It requires a nuanced, patient approach, getting at concrete facts at a time and pace that is comfortable for the participants and as needed to tell their stories in a way that is meaningful to them. Don't worry—yet—about specific facts that may be necessary to ensure complete understanding. If you do become a little lost, you can insert gently phrased clarifying questions, such as the following:

- "Can you help me understand what you meant when you said…?"
- "If I may, I missed what you said about… Can you repeat that last thought?"
- "You just used a term I'm not familiar with and that may be new to [the other participant]. I want to be sure we understand, so could you clarify that term?"
- "Just so I understand where you are going with this, are you saying that…?"

Make your inquiries gentle, slight, and rare so you don't unduly distract them. If you inadvertently do so, apologize and guide them back:

- "I'm sorry; I just needed to understand that point a little better. Thank you for the clarification. Now, you were saying—please continue."

This does not mean you can't ask questions to understand essential facts, particularly where the person has overlooked or avoided them. Ensure that they have fully told the story they need to tell and feel understood, and then ask if you may inquire about these details:

- "Brandon, I think I have a good understanding of your situation. Thank you for sharing it. I do have a few questions just so I understand some of the details you mentioned. Do you mind?"

Or you can suggest that the other participant make these inquiries:

- "Spencer, Brandon has shared a lot of information. Before you provide your own perspective, I'd like to give you the opportunity to ask Brandon about his position, if there is anything that is unclear to you. Will that be okay, Brandon?"

The who, what, and why may then be asked, but in the context of seeking clarification based on the storyteller's path, not giving them the third degree.

Empathizing vs. Identifying
It is human to want to identify with the stories that others tell us. A common way to do this is to share our own stories to signal that we understand what they are experiencing:

- "Oh, I had a similar experience. What happened was…"
- "I completely get where you are coming from. The other day…"
- "Me too! You won't believe what happened to me."

We may have the best intentions, but we are taking the person down our path rather than helping them explore theirs. If one participant does this to the other, ask the person to hold off: "Jerry, I appreciate that you are connecting with what Elaine is saying. Let's be sure she's had the chance to fully share her perspective [or story] first."

Trying to Fix Things
It is natural to want to jump right in and solve a problem. Serving as decision-makers in other roles, we want to offer

advice and direction regarding how participants should approach their conflict or steps they might take. If this is you, avoid practices that may suggest efforts to direct, solve, or judge the situation rather than help others decide for themselves, such as the following:

1. **Advising:** "What you should do is…"
2. **Commanding:** "You had better…"
3. **Diagnosing:** "Your problem is that you…" "You're just feeling guilty about…"
4. **Discounting:** "It can't be all that bad."
5. **Judging:** "That was a silly idea."
6. **Lecturing:** "Don't you know that…"
7. **Preaching:** "You ought to know better than to…" "If you were being honest, you would…"

Support Effective Intercultural Communication

Learning to communicate across different thinking styles, expressions, and responses is a lifelong journey. Mediators can only scratch the surface of intercultural dynamics, so staying vigilant about biases and assumptions is key. Misunderstandings are inevitable, making awareness and adaptability essential. Miscues are bound to happen. For example:

- June avoids eye contact, seeming disinterested, despite your encouragement for open communication. In a private meeting, she insists that she is listening. You realize, to your chagrin, that maintaining eye contact contradicts her cultural norms—she was showing deference, not disrespect, to both her senior coworker and you.
- Hank's loud, direct speech feels "curt" and "rude" to Sally, despite his efforts to moderate it. Frustrated,

he admits that he's worked on this "all my adult life." You shift focus to help Sally express concerns nonjudgmentally so Hank can receive them without offense, while Hank continues adjusting his tone with her.

Let's examine some of the fault lines where intercultural miscues can happen and consider some approaches for minimizing or correcting them.

Understand Low- and High-Context Cultural Influences
Communication theorists speak in terms of low-context and high-context cultures.[8] People with low-context cultural influences communicate with less consideration and need for significant context involving the dynamics of their interpersonal relationships, whereas this broader context matters greatly for people with high-context cultural influences.

Effective listening requires attention to three key aspects of communication: the words spoken, the nonverbal cues that shape their meaning (e.g., facial expressions and body language), and the paraverbal elements that add emphasis, including tone, inflection, pitch, and rhythm. These are vital components for effective listening, and we do well in our efforts to understand another person by attending to each of these aspects.

However, focusing on the message alone won't tell you much about the deeper context of the relationship involved, such as the history of that relationship, how the individuals have managed their conflict in the past, how one individual relates to another based on social, familial, or cultural expectations, or how they each perceive that their conflict should be managed based on these expectations. This is the contrast between low-context communicators, who place less emphasis on these considerations, and high-context communicators, who place more emphasis.

We must not rely on convenient labels to identify any participant as exclusively low or high context. Participants aren't strictly low- or high-context communicators; many adapt their style based on circumstances. However, recognizing their general tendencies helps bridge communication gaps.

Understand Individualistic and Relational Cultural Mindsets

A low-context cultural orientation is often linked to an individualistic mindset, whereas a high-context orientation aligns with a relational mindset. Individualistic communicators focus on the message itself, sharing limited information strategically in order to maintain leverage. As negotiators, they are selective and cautious, with an adversarial approach that prioritizes their own outcomes over those of others or the relationship.

Individualistically minded individuals tend to view themselves as unique and able to function independently without deeper appreciation for living in interdependent relationships. They can "do it myself" or "go it alone." They don't feel constrained by social, cultural, familial, and other relational barriers to get what they want, nor are they as thoughtful about how their actions may impact others based on these relational considerations.

Relationally oriented individuals view communication, conflict resolution, and negotiation as dependent on their relationships with others, including those they feel responsible for. Their decisions are often shaped by social, cultural, and familial obligations. For example, gender and family norms may influence a second daughter to defer to family wishes, whereas a first son may have more independence.

They see themselves as part of a community, unlike individualistic people who view themselves as unique. Relational individuals feel that they must adjust to their circumstances rather than control or change their environment.

With a high-context communication style, relational individuals prioritize building relationships and understanding others' perspectives before negotiating outcomes. They are open to sharing concerns and aim to find mutually satisfying solutions. They also consider the impacts on those they are responsible for, sometimes pausing negotiations to consult with relevant parties.

Manage the Cultural Mix and Bridge the Divide
When we mediate, we must recognize the cultural mix and facilitate processes that balance this mix to ensure that all participants feel fully heard, can fully participate, and can achieve the most beneficial outcomes possible, regardless of the cultural influences at play. We can bridge the divide through practices that help them understand each other more authentically.

> **1. Explore mediation expectations.** One participant may treat the process as a negotiation, withholding information, while the other wants open communication. Reinforce goals for collaboration and set realistic expectations for both participants.
> **2. Explore communication norms.** Consider starting with silence to set a calm pace and give participants time to reflect before responding. Explore how each signals listening such as through eye contact, head nods, or simply looking down in deference to the person speaking. Discuss preferences for tone and volume to both avoid misinterpretations and set clear communication expectations.

3. **Inquire about past conflict resolution.** Learn how participants typically resolve conflicts in order to manage expectations. Use past experiences to guide them through a new process, emphasizing the value of vulnerability and third-party support.
4. **Clarify key terms.** Ask participants to define terms such as "fairness" and "respect" to avoid any misunderstanding. Ensure clarity, especially when terms such as "discrimination" are used in accusations.
5. **Be open to rituals.** Pay attention to rituals that help participants express connection and closure, such as handshakes, stories, or shared hymns, as they can be vital in smoothing the resolution process.
6. **Balance messages of power.** Inquire how participants prefer to be addressed so as to avoid subtle power imbalances, especially when titles are used to assert dominance. If there is an issue, you may need to balance the power, as in this example:
   - Mediator: "Can we go by first names during our mediation today?"
   - Participant with lesser power: "That's fine."
   - Participant with more power: "I'd prefer that you refer to me as 'Dr. Grant.'"
   - Mediator: "Okay, then we'll refer to Mary as 'Ms. Richards' and please refer to me as 'Ms. Ricardo.'"

Whenever a participant inappropriately asserts power, we must minimize the impacts of such messages so that the interests of individuals in lesser power are not compromised.

Stay Present for Difficult Conversations

Everyday difficult conversations often arise when someone's values, identity, or sense of morality are challenged. These may involve social-identity issues such as race, gender, or sexual orientation and perceptions of bias. They can also include attacks on work ethic, integrity, performance, or judgment, often leading to accusations being fired back. Persistent personality clashes are also common. These conversations are difficult because participants are deeply attached to their positions and fail to appreciate others' perspectives. Challenges feel like threats, triggering defensive responses that hinder listening and understanding. Emotions run high, trust is low, and conceding even a small point feels like failure.

When mediating deep conflicts, we may need to rethink "success." Though it's tempting to achieve clear, tidy outcomes, such results may be unrealistic in the moment, especially with limited time and intense clashes. This doesn't mean mediation is unsuccessful. When full resolution isn't possible in the time available, it's good to focus on giving participants space to process their conflicts, believing that resolution is still achievable. Often, resolution comes later through their own efforts, after the mediator's involvement ends.

To maintain both participants' motivation and your faith in the possibility of eventual resolution, you must stay present. Here are the considerations for doing this:

1. Embrace difficult conversations. Avoid shutting them down; discomfort often leads to resolution. Don't moderate to ease your own anxiety—let the dialogue unfold.

2. Address injustice. Acknowledge real or perceived unfairness. Avoid enforcing politeness at the cost of silencing difficult truths or reinforcing power imbalances.

3. Accept your limits. You won't always know how to respond. Stay patient, model composure, and focus on guiding the conversation without forcing direction.

4. Recognize biases. Acknowledge your blind spots. Self-awareness helps prevent biases from interfering with mediation.
5. Show vulnerability. You don't need all the answers. Instead of saying, "I understand," express a willingness to learn: "I don't understand, but I want to."
6. Validate experiences. Even if you question someone's interpretation, prioritize empathy over interrogation. Seek clarity with care.
7. Prioritize listening. When a message is hard to hear, encourage full attention before responding. Clarify what was heard to ensure understanding.
8. Manage overreactions. Strong emotions may be expressed harshly. Don't soften the message to protect the recipient. Facilitate understanding instead.
9. Allow emotional expression. Set reasonable limits but also tolerate outbursts, raised voices, and frustration as part of authentic dialogue.

Your presence anchors the process. We must learn to truly sit with others in these ways. Practice empathic listening in everyday life—be it with a troubled teenager, a stressed employee, or a worried friend. Resist the urge to offer solutions. The more you practice this, the more comfortable you'll become in mediation, where listening and presence are key. It's about valuing others' ability to find their own solutions rather than prioritizing your own.

Sitting with others is like a dance. It is a back-and-forth process of spending time with each participant to hear and reflect on their concerns, encouraging each other to do the same, and checking in to ensure that each person feels fully heard. At times, the dance is awkward and tedious, with beginners stepping on one another's toes. Other times, it is more fluid and natural, involving more seasoned performers. Participants may be able to demonstrate listening and understanding effectively, while at other times the mediator must do the heavy lifting. Either way, it will allow you to be present and sit with them so that you then can share the ride.

Chapter 5 Reflective Exercise

Capture Stories for Future Exploration

As you sit with participants and listen to their stories, track the underlying issues at the heart of the dispute. Frame competing concerns clearly, showing their perspectives, their differences, and how both must work to resolve them.

Tips:

1. **Take notes, but don't be obsessive about it.**
   - Draw a line down the middle of a page; write one person's name at the top of the left column and the other's name at the top of the right column.
   - As the first participant shares, write key points in the appropriate column.
   - Write the other's counterpoints to these issues in the other column. (Ensuring that they match across the columns, point to counterpoint, may not always be possible.)
   - Rather than write in complete sentences, short phrases or bullets will do.
   - The goal is to capture key issues and keep in mind the salient issues and how they differ between the individuals, as well as where there may be common ground, without fussing with formality, order, or neatness.
   - Practice deep listening and avoid constantly looking down at the page.

2. Err on the side of listening and relying on your memory rather than recording items precisely.
- As you later attempt to frame the issues, the participants will let you know when you don't quite have it right.

3. Keep track of basic interests expressed by each participant.
- As you capture participants' respective stories, a picture forms of the central underlying interests at the heart of the dispute.
- Get a sense of the specific interests that each is expressing. Participants often express their concerns in black-and-white terms, suggesting the correctness of their own view and fallacies in the other's.
- Capturing their respective interests, how they differ, and how those differences drive the dispute will help you later frame the issues in a way that provides clarity and guides participants to find a means for addressing their differences.

Fourth Practice: Sit with Others

Participant A: _____	Participant B: _____
Notes, issues, concerns, key points, etc. (add bullets as needed):	**Notes, issues, concerns, key points, etc. (add bullets as needed):**
Participant A's interests (add bullets as needed):	**Participant B's interests (add bullets as needed):**

Chapter 6

Fifth Practice: Share the Ride

*Ceaselessly Support Others Through
the Long Journey to Reconciliation*

"We are in this together, and we are going to be okay."

Chapter Goals

By the end of this chapter, you will:

- understand how to facilitate meaningful dialogue and understanding between participants,
- become more attuned to responding to unproductive reactions and behaviors, and
- be ready to guide participants to collaborative mindsets and responses.

The process for "sitting with others" described in the last chapter seems simple enough. One person speaks, the other listens, then switch. The mediator engages when participants aren't respecting this process and continues until they stop interrupting one another. Yet, in reality, it is rarely that simple.

People in conflict don't always know the most effective or artful ways to communicate. They can say or do things that cause offense, then take offense themselves when confronted by similar gaffes. Everyday mediators find ways to smooth out the bumps and rough edges. They keep people at the table, helping each communicate in ways that the other will understand and appreciate. They emphasize dialogue over debate and help individuals adjust their communication practices so they don't shut down or erupt in anger and frustration.

The bus ride of interpersonal conflict may, at times, be arduous and tense, and everyday mediators commit to the long journey to help individuals talk through their concerns and identify the most important issues in need of resolution. Put simply, they share the ride with them.

A Story: "Share the Ride" in Action

Ricardo is a well-respected mediator specializing in domestic cases and civil suits involving contracts, negligence, and employment. Known for his legal expertise and ability to facilitate collaborative outcomes, he is often referred to by judges and attorneys seeking to resolve disputes outside the courtroom. However, he was surprised to receive a call from Thomas, a partner at a large firm, requesting mediation for a sensitive interpersonal conflict between two senior partners, Judith and Rex.

Judith, a managing partner responsible for personnel matters, had recently implemented a firm decision to place Rex on unpaid leave for two months due to gross misconduct linked to alcohol abuse. He was given an ultimatum to seek treatment, make amends, and change his behavior or risk being terminated.

Thomas acknowledged that Rex had made progress—seeking addiction counseling, apologizing to colleagues, and demonstrating a more tempered demeanor. However, Judith remained skeptical, viewing his transformation as another manipulative act. She was pushing to extend his leave, unwilling to reinstate him without further assurances. Thomas was in a difficult position, valuing both Judith's

Fifth Practice: Share the Ride

leadership and Rex's legal prowess, and feared losing Judith if the situation were mishandled.

Ricardo agreed to mediate, beginning with separate meetings with each party. Rex, tough and defensive, often fought with words, a skill honed in the courtroom. However, Ricardo had also seen Rex relent after a settlement had been reached and litigation avoided. Rex admitted to Ricardo that his life was in turmoil, and he had much to lose if he couldn't resolve things.

"What's holding you back?" Ricardo asked.

"She has this picture of the model attorney who can be aggressive when he needs to be but is otherwise charming and complacent, even genteel, in interactions with just about anyone—even assholes. That's just not me, even when I'm sober. I may be a bastard, but it's why I'm a successful lawyer."

Ricardo saw Rex's conflict style as competitive and compromising. He pushed hard to win but only relented when there was something to lose, such as face or status. What was missing was the willingness to accommodate others' needs, especially in relationships, which Rex struggled with, particularly with Judith. Judith, on the other hand, was calm, controlled, and nonreactive, able to maintain composure while making reasoned, respectful arguments to move others toward agreement—qualities Rex lacked, especially when emotions would run high.

Only in private, after the "fight," would she reveal frustration and anxiety. "I'm not going to let down my guard with Rex," she said, "no matter what you may expect."

"I don't expect anything," said Ricardo. "It all depends on what you and Rex are willing to do."

"Well, I'm through with his courtroom tactics and bullying. I'm the lone holdout regarding Rex's return. They want me to let Rex off the hook, yet again. That's what Tom wants.

And I say if that's the case, fine, but not without a cost. I'll leave."

"Which Tom doesn't want either."

"Well," Judith said with no further response. Ricardo sensed a brief loss of composure, as though she were about to shed a tear before collecting herself. It really wasn't "fine" for her. She really didn't want to leave the firm, even though other firms would hire her in an instant.

Ricardo saw Judith's conflict style as more nuanced than Rex's. Though she had a competitive streak, honed by years of legal practice, she preferred collaboration and finding solutions. She excelled at settlement negotiations, engaging respectfully and aiming for win-win outcomes. However, her desire to avoid conflict personally, while fighting professionally, was pushing her to a breaking point with Rex. Most colleagues met her expectations, but Rex's resistance could force her to leave, a decision that would devastate the firm.

Ricardo believed that a compromise would surface, with Rex regulating his behavior in order to be allowed to return and Judith agreeing to reinstate him. But compromise would only result in surface-level compliance, leading to quiet resentment until a blowup would ultimately occur. Rex would eventually break Judith's expectations, and she would continue tolerating it, compromising her own values, while feeling the pressure from the firm's partners.

Rex and Judith needed to stop "lawyering" their relationship and explore the deeper values and needs. Ricardo didn't have an easy solution but felt better equipped, knowing more about their relationship and how they each responded to conflict. He trusted that the answers would come in the dialogue that would be promoted during mediation.

Promote Dialogue over Discussion and Debate

Interpersonal communication is a multifaceted process, shaped by nuances, complexities, and individual differences. In both personal and professional settings, how we engage with others can significantly impact the outcomes of our interactions. Instead of relying solely on discussion or debate, which often prioritize winning or proving a point, promoting dialogue fosters mutual understanding, empathy, and collaboration. It encourages a shared exploration of ideas, where all voices are valued, leading to deeper connections and more constructive solutions. In this context, cultivating the skills to engage in meaningful dialogue is essential for effective communication and relationship-building.

Think about conversations among close friends. Interruptions, tangents, and heated arguments often occur, but they quickly settle down with laughter and understanding. When asked what they were fighting about, they'll say they weren't fighting at all—it's just how they talk. On the other hand, you might overhear a polite conversation between two people who seem comfortable, only to realize they are both seething with anger and unable to express their true feelings. What gives?

The difference is dialogue. It may not always be pretty or meet your expectations for proper conversation, but we must be patient with it if it advances understanding. As you mediate, observe:

- When are people finding their way, even though they appear to be fighting?
- When could they stand to be a little less polite, risking a fight for the sake of communicating more clearly and honestly?

- When do we need to realize that some will fight as they enter mediation and continue afterwards, with nothing seemingly resolved, and that the best we can do is help them identify skills and strategies for "fighting better"?

At the core, we need to recognize three fundamentally different communication processes at work when people talk: (1) polite but unproductive discussion, (2) all-out argument and debate, and (3) engaged and fruitful (though not always comfortable) dialogue.[9]

Polite but Unproductive Discussion

We are often conditioned to be polite in conversations, even when we're frustrated or feel unheard, while not necessarily being open to others' perspectives. Unlike in a debate, we're not trying to defeat others, but we're also not willing to let go of our own positions, such as in a discussion. The Greek root *cus*, meaning "to shake apart,"[10] appears in both "discussion" and words such as "percussion" and "concussion," which involve a clash or impact—one loud, the other painful. Discussion, often the default mode, can seem respectful but often ends up being a clash of opinions without meaningful resolution.

Individuals engaged in this form of conversation tend to do the following:

- Defend their positions through persuasion, presentation of ideas, and respectful argument
- Politely acknowledge others' concerns without ultimately giving them much credence
- Respond to inquiries and provide information in further defense of their positions

- Present positions as "either/or" propositions, suggesting that differing positions are not valid
- Allow opportunity for others to speak but with no true intent to listen, often continuing to defend their positions and refuting others'
- Gain agreement through persuasion that may or may not be the product of full deliberation or consideration of all perspectives
- Leave the discussion with the same perspectives and positions as when they entered, little persuaded by the presentation of other perspectives

All-Out Argument and Debate
Debate, in this context, isn't about the structured, respectful exchanges learned in debate class. Instead, it often involves shouting matches, personal attacks, and dismissing opposing arguments, with the goal not of presenting valid insights but rather of defeating the opponent at all costs. In our media-driven culture, such behavior has become the norm, transforming debate into the default mode for everyday discourse.

Individuals engaged in this form of conversation, if we may call it that, tend to do the following:

- Push for a "win" at the cost of relationships and without concern for others' perspectives or feelings
- Emphasize disagreement between their and others' positions, stressing the flaws in others' arguments and the correctness of their own
- Seek to defeat others' arguments through personal and demeaning attacks and manipulative tactics
- Provide self-justifying rationale for their positions rather than a thoughtful or logical defense

- Present arguments in an "either/or" framework that provides no space for viewpoints or positions contrary to their own

Engaged and Fruitful (Though Not Always Comfortable) Dialogue

In dialogue, we express our concerns knowing that others may disagree yet will listen, ask thoughtful questions, and offer differing views without dismissing ours. Though mediation requires decisions to move forward, the goal is to understand each other's role in the conflict and challenges in relating to one another. By taking time to consider others' viewpoints without reacting or rushing to judgment, we can ensure that everyone feels heard, respected, and satisfied that the decisions made address concerns from all sides.

Dialogue requires time to uncover deeper concerns, which polite discussion or debate rarely achieves. It can be uncomfortable, not because we defend ourselves but because it forces us to confront our own limitations and contributions. True dialogue only happens in safe environments where people can open up without fear of judgment, attack, or diminishing criticism.

Individuals engaged in this form of conversation tend to do the following:

- Listen and seek to understand others' viewpoints without an intent to respond or offer a defense
- Seek opportunities for agreement and connection between differing perspectives
- Inquire into others' assumptions that support their positions and are equally open to receiving inquiry about their own assumptions

- View the process as an opportunity to learn through inquiry and disclosure without an immediate intent to push toward a decision
- Search for collective meaning among divergent viewpoints
- Perceive opportunities for "both/and" outcomes that incorporate as best as possible the positions and interests of all

When mediation participants are engaged in dialogue, you will find yourself sitting back and allowing the conversation to unfold. When they aren't, you will become more involved. It starts with better understanding their conflict behaviors.

Observe and Understand Participants' Conflict Behaviors

Everyday mediators must observe participants' behaviors, responses to conflict, and emotional influences in order to develop strategies for fostering more productive collaboration. Though we all adapt our behaviors to fit a situation, we tend to rely on preferred "default" styles. However, these defaults may not always be effective. Using the wrong tool for the job, such as always relying on a hammer when a different tool is needed, leads to disappointing results unless we become more aware of when our default behaviors help or hinder us in specific conflicts.

Many, including myself, tend to avoid conflict because it's difficult to confront others about hurtful behaviors. Though avoiding conflict can be justified at times, it often doesn't lead to the best outcomes. To achieve better results, it's important to adapt your behaviors and become more responsive, even if it's uncomfortable.

We can help mediation participants understand their own behaviors in the midst of conflict so they can be more responsive in addressing it. This raises two questions:

1. What are the participants' tendencies or default behaviors when responding to most conflicts?

2. Are those tendencies or default behaviors serving them in the current conflict? If not, what different strategies and approaches might they adopt in order to be more effective in addressing the current conflict?

As you work with participants, look for the following clues about the individuals:

- Is one more timid and reserved?
- Is the other brash and overbearing?
- Is one excessively argumentative?
- Is the other dismissive and sarcastic?
- How are they asserting power and position or seeking to protect themselves from such assertions?
- What behaviors are you observing that suggest that one of them feels fearful or threatened?
- Where might they be offering concessions and opportunities for compromise?

Recognize and Respond to Fear (Fight or Flight)
There are many reasons behind conflict behaviors,[11] and fear is a common one. In mediation, people often fear losing something tangible, such as money or relationships, or something intangible, such as their reputation or dignity. They may also fear retaliation, humiliation, or embarrassment. Though the underlying causes may not always be

clear, signs of fear, anxiety, or being overwhelmed often indicate a "fight-or-flight" response, which is an instinctive reaction to a perceived threat that triggers immediate self-protective behavior.[12] In mediation, these responses arise when one person's words or actions leave the other feeling attacked, vulnerable, or diminished, leading to emotional reactions such as anger, hurt, confusion, or anxiety.

"Fight" responses can appear in the form of aggressive and competitive behaviors as individuals become argumentative, raise their voices, engage in verbal attacks and debate tactics, and demonstrate other overt behaviors as a means of overcoming the threat. Further examples include the following:

- **Attack.** Responding with an intent to hurt the other person.
- **Argue.** Arguing past the other person without acknowledging the validity of their arguments or viewpoints.
- **Debate.** Escalating the conflict with the intent to defeat the other person's arguments and possibly attack their character.
- **Shock and confusion.** Expressing surprise at a comment or action that hurt you, pronouncing it offensive and signaling uncertainty about how to respond.
- **Label.** Describing the other person's behavior or statement—or the person—in less-than-flattering terms.

"Flight" responses can appear in the form of avoidant and accommodating behaviors as individuals seek to escape or minimize a threat by becoming withdrawn or quiet, making quick concessions against their interests, displaying passive nonverbals such as downward eye gazes or heavy sighs, or making mollifying statements when their dejected body language suggests otherwise. Further examples:

- **Leave.** Physically removing ourselves from a situation that makes us uncomfortable.
- **Avoid.** Withdrawing emotionally from people or situations that cause us to feel hurt or anxious.
- **Silence.** Staying in the room, enduring a hurtful situation without saying or doing anything.
- **Ignore.** Choosing to let go of or not be bothered by a situation that hurts us.
- **Deflect.** Changing the subject or responding in an unexpected way, such as through humor or sarcasm.
- **Give in.** Conceding, often with statements we don't mean, such as "that's okay," "it doesn't matter," "I don't mind," etc.

Though these triggers and our responses to them can jeopardize the mediation process, addressing them appropriately provides opportunities for returning individuals to more-collaborative approaches. In many cases, as mediator, you can simply acknowledge the trigger and then return to substantive discussions. For example:

- **Name it.** "I wonder if Bill's comment a minute ago is leaving you confused and not knowing how to respond."
- **Confront it.** "Your comment to Sally seems a little harsh. I don't see how it will help the situation."
- **Strategize.** "How would you like to respond to Peter and let him know that his actions are making you not want to continue discussions?"

- **Mirror nonverbals.** "You say that the proposal is okay with you. But you don't seem that happy about it, so I wonder if the proposal really isn't okay."
- **Educated guess.** "I could be mistaken, so please tell me otherwise, but you seem (upset, disappointed, withdrawn, etc.). Is that what's happening? Is there anything you can share so I can help you?"

Your job is to observe statements, actions, and behaviors, and how participants respond to them, in order to engage participants in strategies in an effort to more constructively manage their conflict. Fear and the associated emotional and psychological threats that cause fear cover a wide range of possibilities for explaining conflict responses. Understanding and addressing fear provide significant opportunities for moving participants toward collaboration.

Move Participants Toward Collaborative Mindsets and Responses

To truly share the ride with others, everyday mediators must do more than promote dialogue and observe conflict behaviors. We need to move the participants along the bumpy road to resolution with collaborative mindsets and responses. Effectively doing so starts with assessing, reflecting, and planning.

Assess, Reflect, and Plan

The process starts by assessing the conflict dynamics, including each participant's needs, perspectives, and goals. Once identified, it's important to plan strategies that encourage open communication, tailored to each participant's response to conflict—whether avoidance, competition, or compromise—creating an environment conducive to collaboration.

Assess

Understanding each participant's conflict tendencies helps you anticipate their reactions during mediation. Preliminary meetings may help, but in some cases, your existing knowledge of the individuals or information gleaned in the early stages of mediation might be enough. Avoid pigeonholing participants. Use conflict tendencies as a guide—not absolutes—and remain open to breaking unproductive patterns.

Reflect

After meeting with participants, reflecting on the deeper issues allows you to visualize potential outcomes—both positive and negative. Though imagining solutions and roadblocks can be helpful, it's important to not immediately act on these reflections. Instead, use them to build a flexible plan that anticipates responses and promotes collaboration.

Plan

Your plan should remain adaptable, as the mediation may unfold unpredictably. However, understanding potential behaviors will also help you prepare your strategy. For instance, if a participant tends to shut down on certain issues, you might need to meet separately and guide them on how to address such topics assertively. If another participant becomes argumentative, you'll be ready to manage that response, ensuring that both sides feel heard and understood.

A Varying Approach

People often enter a conflict with preconceived views of the situation, believing that their needs are incompatible with those of the other person. However, in reality, they rely on each other to meet those needs, which is what makes the conflict meaningful. Regardless of how they each respond to conflict, our role is to help participants see the value of collaboration as the best way to address their needs. We need to guide them toward a collaborative mindset and demonstrate the power of dialogue.

How you move participants toward collaboration depends on the situation and may require private conversations, group discussions, or a mix of both. Your approach will vary based on the conflict response exhibited and the timing within the mediation process. The conflict response could be fight (competing), flight (avoiding and accommodating), or compromise.

Flight Conflict Response (Avoiding and Accommodating Behaviors)

Individuals who avoid conflict escape having to assert their own interests or consider others' needs, instead opting not to engage. Though this may be sensible to prevent discussing trivial matters, avoidance does not help mediation participants resolve their concerns that are far from trivial. In fact, they may have arrived at mediation because they have finally come to understand the cost of their avoidance.

Accommodating individuals prioritize others' needs, valuing relationships over outcomes. In negotiations, they may concede points in order to build trust. However, excessive accommodation can enable others to take advantage of and mistreat them.

Whether avoidant or accommodating, they need guidance in asserting their needs, helping them balance listening, concessions, and self-advocacy.

Pre-Mediation Conversations

People avoid raising concerns due to fear of negative reactions, past hostility, or potential retaliation—or because they feel that speaking up won't make a difference. In pre-mediation meetings, build rapport and address these fears to anticipate challenges. Assure participants that you'll help them voice their concerns and manage any reactions from the other person.

If the person opens up, acknowledge their clarity and confidence, reinforcing their ability to express concerns in mediation. Ask, "What keeps you from sharing these concerns as you have with me?" to explore barriers and find ways to support them.

Accommodators act out of kindness and respect, which should be acknowledged, but they must also voice their own needs. Ask, "Do you feel confident raising your concerns? Why or why not?" Assess whether accommodation stems from pressure or power dynamics rather than natural tendencies. Explore fears about mediation or the other party's receptiveness.

Offer participants in flight mode general strategies for assertive, nonjudgmental communication. Walk through scenarios, help refine their approach, and suggest preparing bullet points to stay focused. Emphasize that this is a rare opportunity to express concerns and encourage reflection on what they stand to lose by staying silent or making concessions against their self-interests.

During Mediation with the Other Participant(s) Present
Mediators must ensure a fair balance of participation, meaning each participant should feel fully heard. This can be challenging if one participant is avoidant or reluctant to speak. Be mindful not to give too much deference to a more talkative participant. If the other participant tends to interrupt or dominate, signal the need to give the avoidant individual time and opportunity to speak. For example: "Thank you, Alan, for sharing your concerns. Let's give Betty similar consideration to express her concerns."

Fifth Practice: Share the Ride

Equal time doesn't mean taking the same approach with all participants. Show sensitivity to the avoidant participant by allowing silence without pressure to fill the space with words. You might say, "Take your time; there's no rush. You can respond whenever you're ready. We'll wait."

If, through no fault of the other person, the avoidant person still isn't speaking up, provide encouragement in a way that won't embarrass the individual: "Maureen, I think Barry has shared a lot regarding his perspective. I'd like to encourage you to do the same, and I think Barry would also like to understand your perspective."

If you sense continued reluctance, a gentle urging may help the participant find the words (and courage) to begin to share concerns, or it may signal a need for a break so you can meet separately with the participant to help address their concerns.

In contrast to avoiders, overly accommodating participants will concede points too quickly and/or acknowledge consent to their clear disadvantage. Intervene tactfully: "Margaret, earlier, you mentioned needing uninterrupted time for projects. Jake agreed 'in theory' but wouldn't guarantee it. You said 'okay,' but is that truly okay with you?"

When the participants let comments go unchallenged, encourage a response: "Izzy, before Harry moves on, do you want to address what he just said?"

Watch for body language signaling discomfort: "Liz, you said 'that's fine,' but I'm sensing that you feel otherwise. Do we need to discuss this?"

Like avoiders, accommodators may be motivated by fear, making concessions in order to avoid conflict, which may also signal a need for a break to discuss the matter privately.

Separate Private Meeting with a Participant During Mediation

One reason for meeting privately is out of concern for embarrassing a participant in front of the other participant or weakening their position. If an avoidant participant struggles to speak up, meet separately to discuss their concerns and help them plan for addressing the issue. Accommodating participants require similar support. For example: "Lawrence, you've been respectful of Etta's stance, but I wonder if you're holding back too much. Do you want help raising your concerns?"

Encourage the participant to voice concerns when returning to mediation, offering reassurance while empowering them to speak for themselves. Before returning, agree on what will be shared and whether they need your support in sharing or will take that responsibility solely on their own.

If another participant's behavior discourages engagement, a private meeting may be needed to address it directly. If the individual can be brought to understand how they are coming across, you can offer some coaching to help them modify these behaviors so the avoidant participant will feel able to open up more. If you sense that a participant's overbearing nature is causing an accommodating participant to acquiesce either to get along or from discomfort or fear, challenge the behavior and encourage a more collaborative approach. Challenge them to consider whether "winning" is worth damaging the relationship.

Fight Conflict Response (Competitive Behaviors)

Competitive individuals often assert their own interests and push to achieve outcomes beneficial for themselves without considering the interests of others or how those outcomes may potentially harm their relationships. When relationships matter as much as, or more than, achieving a particular outcome, such people must learn to relax their grip. We must help them see how aggressive posturing and a failure to consider others' interests can result in achieving less-successful outcomes for themselves.

Pre-Mediation Conversations
Competitive communication is often learned—and used to gain attention, rewards, or dominance. It can stem from fear, masked by argumentation and assertiveness. Observe interruptions and reactive tendencies and gently highlight how they hinder understanding. Model active listening and encourage reflection: "What do you hope to achieve? How might this impact your relationship?"

If fear triggers reactivity, explore underlying concerns and help normalize emotional responses while emphasizing their impact on communication. Ask the participants how you can help them during mediation to remain calm, reflective, and less reactive.

During Mediation with the Other Participant(s) Present
Competitive behaviors—interrupting, talking over, and arguing—often require immediate intervention. Remind participants of agreed norms: "Nick, I know Zach's remarks upset you, but take a moment, think about what was said, and respond in a way he can better understand."

Sometimes, tone, manner, or choice of words will call for a response: "Jack, you say you support Diane's proposal, but do I detect sarcasm? How can Diane know that you are being sincere?" Immediately stop offensive comments: "Sammy, insults like 'you're stupid' violate the respect rule."

In the face of persistent disruptive behavior, suggest taking a break: "Stacey, could we discuss something in the hallway?"

Separate Private Meeting with a Participant During Mediation

If competition persists, privately address behaviors with firm but supportive guidance: "I've asked you to stop interrupting Louise. It's frustrating her and blocking resolution. Do you not want to reach an agreement?"

Help strategize ways to rebuild trust: "Ronald, I appreciate your effort to be less argumentative. How can we show Margaret that you're serious?"

People in fight mode feel no less fearful than avoidant and accommodating individuals do. Be attuned to any acknowledgement about how they come across and use their openness as an opportunity to support more productive behaviors back in the room.

At the same time, help the other participant navigate competitive behaviors without derailing the process:

- "Karen, Mike is working on being less argumentative. Keep sharing your concerns, and I'll make sure he stays on track."
- "Bob, Suzanne reacts negatively whenever you mention the cat incident. Might your sarcasm be triggering her anger?"

Compromise Conflict Response

Compromise is often the default in negotiations, providing partial satisfaction and helping to maintain relationships. It works well for practical needs in business or daily life but differs from true collaboration. Though mediators rely on compromise, it can feel unsatisfying when lasting peace and reconciliation are the goals. If participants settle but are open to more, mediators should push to explore better solutions that support long-term cooperation.

Pre-Mediation Conversations

Compromisers share certain traits with accommodators, requiring similar encouragement to help others reach a resolution, but differ in their desire to meet their own interests. Whereas accommodators often say, "That's okay; they can have that," compromisers say, "If I can get this, they can have that." The accommodator gives while the compromiser gives and takes. When working with compromisers, support their instinct to resolve the issue while at the same time challenging them to aim for more than just settling.

If a participant is hesitant to share their deepest goals and interests in mediation, explore what it will mean to them if they remain unaddressed. Do they feel that the goals they've achieved so far are enough? Will they be satisfied if only some of their goals are achieved, or will doubts remain? Is there a risk of revisiting the conflict if certain issues remain unresolved?

If a participant acknowledges that a compromise wouldn't fully satisfy them, remind them that your role is to help participants communicate in ways they haven't before. Explore what has held them back from a better result and a stronger relationship.

Your goal is to help the participants move beyond their limitations. This is especially crucial in long-term relationships where a participant may feel sadness about not reaching a more collaborative resolution. It's not therapy but rather an opportunity to help them communicate more clearly with your support. Be ready to interject the right tools and/or strategies whenever these moments arise during mediation.

During Mediation with the Other Participant(s) Present

When participants reach a compromise, acknowledge their progress and celebrate their successes: "Neil and Patrick, you've made great strides in agreeing on issues such as the fence, the tree, and noise. I'll include these in the final agreement. Great job!"

Then look for further collaboration opportunities.

If the issue is more emotional than substantive, gently probe deeper: "Tricia, though Pauline's offer seems reasonable, is there more to it? Are you still concerned about how she interacts with you?"

Help participants explore deeper issues beyond surface-level compromise, especially when the true consequences aren't fully considered, and encourage participants to reflect on the potential relationship benefits or losses.

If necessary, be direct about the crucial decision point: "I'm hearing reluctance to address the core issue. Jerry, Tom, your tensions remain unresolved, and it's costing you both. Can we work through this honestly?"

Finally, encourage participants to lean on your support for tough discussions: "I know this is difficult, but that's why I'm here. You've trusted me to help you navigate these challenges, and I believe we can reach an outcome that benefits both of you."

Separate Private Meeting with a Participant During Mediation

In some cases, it might be better to address certain issues privately with a participant before doing so in front of both parties, depending on the context. For example, if Tom has expressed concerns privately with you about how unfairly he feels he's been treated, it could be helpful to ask, "Tom, you've agreed to rehab and amends, but you also want Jerry to understand how hurt you've been by some of his accusations about your behavior. Do you want to raise that before we finish today?"

If a matter is too delicate or could embarrass someone, that could also prompt a separate meeting. Or a separate meeting might be called for when a participant is about to settle for a compromise that goes against their interests.

You might also meet separately if one participant is minimizing the relationship value for a tangible outcome. For example: "Lori, Felicity is asking for more understanding about the challenges she faces with parenting. Do you want to give that more consideration?" If one participant is being impatient or aggressive, again, consider a private meeting to explore their approach.

Finally, if Jerry wants to conclude mediation but there's still unresolved tension, ask, "Jerry, you've been generous, but would it hurt to hear Tom out a little longer about why he feels that things haven't been fair?"

By facilitating meaningful dialogue, we see how sharing the ride with genuine understanding between participants can shift the conversation from defensiveness to collaboration. When we respond to unproductive reactions and behaviors, we help to ensure that emotional barriers are addressed and that every voice is heard as we guide participants toward collaborative mindsets,[13] where both their needs and those of others can be met in a way that supports long-term cooperation. Together, this will lead to the next stop along *The Mediation Road Map*, where we truly see the transformative power of mediation.

Chapter 6 Reflective Exercise

Assess/Reflect/Plan Road Map

Whether taking notes or planning in your head during the time you have before mediating, use this tool to help you anticipate participant behaviors and responses and develop a fluid plan for the tools, strategies, and approaches you may need to call upon to "share the ride" with participants and move them toward collaboration. If you need help getting started, please see the example in the resources section at the end of the book.

Assess
What am I observing about each participant's behaviors and conflict styles? How do they respond when challenged? What are the consistent patterns that keep each stuck in conflict? (Note: consider fight, flight, or compromise responses or describe participant behaviors in other ways that you find helpful.)

Participant:
- Behavior/Attribute Style
- Behavior/Attribute Style
- Behavior/Attribute Style

Participant:
- Behavior/Attribute Style
- Behavior/Attribute Style
- Behavior/Attribute Style

Reflect
What are the situations and scenarios in which the participants clashed before? What was happening? How did each respond? What situations might arise in mediation? How

might these situations threaten possibilities for collaboration? How might they present opportunities?

Participant:
- Notes
- Notes

Participant:
- Notes
- Notes

Plan

What skills, approaches, and strategies might I need to respond to the behaviors and situations I've described? (Think in terms of specific scenarios and the particular skill, approach, or strategy you may need to use. Keep the plan flexible in order to prepare for matters you won't be able to anticipate.)

Participant:
- Skill/Approach
- Skill/Approach
- Skill/Approach

Participant:
- Skill/Approach
- Skill/Approach
- Skill/Approach

Chapter 7

Sixth Practice: Bring Transformative Power

Find, Support, and Exploit Breakthrough Moments

"Let's work together and find a way forward."

Chapter Goals

By the end of this chapter, you will:

- understand how to frame issues for effective problem-solving,
- recognize how to utilize interest-based negotiation strategies and techniques, and
- lean into pushing and pulling participants toward breakthrough.

Everyday mediators understand those moments when it feels like mediation is getting nowhere. They realize that exhaustion, ambiguity, and contention present both risks for ending mediation without resolution and opportunities for breakthrough and reconciliation.

As we discussed in chapter 6, our power is in being present in these moments as we share the participants' journey. We must persevere, encouraging participants to keep exploring pathways to resolution, challenging them when they don't want to move forward, hypothesizing a better world if they reach resolution, and considering what they may regret if they end too soon or too short of a better outcome. When we do so, there is truly transformative power in our everyday mediations.

A Story: "Bring Transformative Power" in Action

Stacy and Annalise were planning a training program at a coffee shop when they unexpectedly saw Lexi, a former coworker who had been promoted years prior. Annalise hoped that Lexi wouldn't see them, but she did, and she suggested that the three of them sit down to discuss an exciting new project. Annalise, still bitter from their past, agreed reluctantly.

After the encounter, Annalise vented to Stacy, expressing her frustration over how when Lexi was still her coworker, she had damaged Annalise's reputation and manipulated situations to her benefit, especially when Annalise had been assigned to work under Lexi's lead on a sales-training project. Though the project had led to Lexi's promotion, Annalise's resentment still lingered.

Stacy had never faced Lexi the way Annalise had. Lexi had ingratiated herself with their former boss, Helena, who treated her like a daughter. Three years ago, Lexi had convinced Helena to assign Annalise to a full-time sales-training project, making Lexi her de facto boss. Annalise felt bullied and her reputation suffered, especially since the project led to Lexi's promotion. Although Lexi eventually left and Helena retired, the experience still stung. The next morning, Stacy ran into Lexi in the parking lot. Lexi asked how Annalise was, noting how quiet she was at the coffee shop. Stacy said that she was doing great, leading high-level projects.

Sixth Practice: Bring Transformative Power

"That's good," Lexi said. "I talked with Gordon about working with her. It's a sales-training initiative. He said to talk with her directly, so I guess that's what I need to do."

Gordon, their new boss, was different from Helena: collaborative, transparent. His insistence that Lexi speak to Annalise herself was refreshing.

"I'm really going to need her for this one," Lexi added. "It's imperative."

Stacy recognized the familiar Lexi-isms: "imperative" meant self-important, and "we" usually meant Annalise doing the work.

Stacy asked exactly what she needed Annalise to do as they walked toward and got into the elevator. When Lexi mentioned that she needed a partner to help develop training, Stacy immediately asked, "How are you planning to ask her?"

"I don't know. I assume we'll meet and discuss it. Why?"

Stacy hesitated. "You'd have to ask her, but I know she's really busy right now."

"Well, she'll have to. It's hugely important. If we fail, we could lose significant market share."

Stacy doubted it. Lexi was prone to catastrophizing. "Well, good luck talking with her," she said as they reached the third floor.

Lexi stopped Stacy, asking to talk more. She knew that Annalise didn't want to work with her but stressed to Stacy that she needed Annalise's expertise. Stacy suggested Lexi speak to Annalise directly, but Lexi hesitated and asked Stacy to mediate. Stacy accepted on the condition that all relevant parties agreed, including Annalise, Gordon, and Lexi's boss, Pratibha. Lexi agreed. Later, Stacy learned that Pratibha had spoken to Gordon, urging Annalise to work with Lexi, though Gordon left the decision to Annalise.

"I don't want to work with that...witch again," Annalise said, always careful with words.

Stacy told her about Lexi's request for mediation. Annalise was skeptical but agreed that a discussion was necessary—especially with Gordon and Pratibha's support.

Stacy, Lexi, and Annalise met a week later. Stacy kept things informal.

"Lexi, why don't you start?"

"I'd rather hear Annalise's concerns first."

"Maybe explain the project in more detail?" Annalise asked.

Lexi complied and Stacy asked Annalise if she had any questions. She didn't, and wanted to move forward, saying she understood the project. Lexi said she had nothing else to add. Annalise folded her arms and looked down. "I have nothing to say at the moment."

An awkward silence. Lexi, as always, maintained her steely, unreadable expression, while Stacy considered Annalise's apprehension. She turned to Annalise. "It's no secret you don't want to work with Lexi again. Wouldn't it help to talk about it?"

Annalise remained silent, but Stacy assured her there was no rush. Finally, Annalise spoke. "Lexi, you said you needed a 'partner.' What do you mean?"

Lexi's tone was clipped. "I need you to develop and deliver training. It's all laid out. Our sales directors agreed that you're the best fit. Don't trust me—ask them."

"So you've decided everything. You just need me to execute?"

"I need you as a 'partner' to develop and deliver sales training." Lexi's sarcasm was unmistakable.

Annalise turned to Stacy. "This is the same nightmare. Lexi's version of 'partnering' is me following her plan exactly, or else it's 'wrong.'"

Sixth Practice: Bring Transformative Power

"That's a start," commented Stacy. "Tell us more."

Annalise hesitated, then slowly opened up. Stacy encouraged her, rephrased key points, and ensured that Lexi had a chance to listen and reflect. When asked to summarize, Lexi responded dryly. "Apparently, I'm a horrible person who won't let Annalise have control."

"I never said that!" Annalise shot back. "Difficult to work with? Yes. And I've explained why."

Lexi defended her approach. "I consult Annalise, use her expertise. But I answer for the final product. Our clients trust me to filter information."

"All after the fact," Annalise interjected. "After you've already decided everything."

Lexi and Annalise debated—Lexi citing business reasons, Annalise countering with the impact. The final blow? Lexi ran to their boss, Helena, instead of addressing concerns directly.

"You ran to 'Momma' and tanked my reputation."

"That's not true," Lexi retorted. "Your version is dramatic and wrong." Frustrated, she continued, "We're not getting anywhere. I thought this was about the project."

Stacy stepped in. "Lexi, you expected a negotiation. Annalise is making it clear this is personal. She wants you to understand the damage."

Annalise scoffed. "More like 'can't understand.' I'm not sure there's a human there."

Lexi smiled for the first time. "So what do we do?"

Stacy answered, "Before we discuss the project, can we agree that you two should even work together?"

Lexi frowned. "I assumed we were. Isn't that the expectation?"

"Is it?" Stacy turned to Annalise.

Annalise took a deep breath. "Everyone assumes that I'll work with Lexi, like it's no big deal. I respect Gordon, but it feels like an expectation." She paused, then continued, "Except, I can refuse. People act like I have no choice, but I do."

Lexi stiffened. "Well, I—I need to talk to Pratibha. This is a waste of time."

"Hold on," Stacy said. "I think you need to hear Annalise out."

Lexi folded her arms. "Okay."

Annalise met Lexi's gaze. "I don't have to do this. People may be upset. I could lose my job. So be it. I won't work with you under these circumstances."

Lexi's composure cracked. "You're making a mistake. This will ruin your career."

Stacy seized on Annalise's phrasing. "'Under these circumstances.' Are there conditions under which you would work with Lexi?"

Annalise laid them out: acknowledgment of past harm, transparency in the project, no undercutting or gatekeeping, and a commitment from Lexi to advocate for these terms with leadership. If not, she'd leave the project—or even the company altogether. Silence stretched. Stacy turned to Lexi. "Do you have any questions? A response?"

Nothing. Lexi sat back, arms crossed, furious. Stacy sighed. "You've got a lot to think about. Can you accept Annalise's terms? If you can't, what does that mean for you?"

She offered to facilitate further discussions but doubted that Lexi would budge. She also doubted that Annalise would lose her job. Mediation couldn't force outcomes. It only provided the space. Annalise had chosen. Now Lexi had to as well.

Frame Issues to Capture Participants' Interests in a Compelling Way

Framing issues is a succinct step in the mediation process wherein the mediator moves the participants from the formal process of storytelling to helping them make sense of their underlying interests and where the variance between their interests lies.

Help Participants Identify Interests Beneath Hard and Fast Positions

People in conflict instinctively hold to hard and fast positions. Though celebrated among trial lawyers, unethical business leaders, and politicians, this adversarial bargaining mindset does not promote positive relationships in which people demonstrate consideration for others' concerns and needs while also advocating for their own.

Understandably, participants are reluctant to consider another person's concerns if they feel that the other person won't reciprocate. Holding to positions creates an unproductive downward spiral, but everyday mediators help participants move from holding positions to communicating and addressing interests. Interests are the needs, goals, values, and other concerns that individuals in conflict wish to have met. A short list of interests includes:

Love	Appreciation	Trust
Security	Self-esteem	Physical needs
Freedom	Privacy	Safety
Relaxation	Understanding	Approval
Consideration	Power	Fun
Order	Friendship	Acceptance
Respect	Competence	Excitement
Control	Comfort	Financial needs

The key to resolution is helping participants articulate their underlying interests rather than rigid positions they hold. People stuck in a "yes or no" mindset struggle to find common ground, but exploring the "why" and "why not" behind their positions can reveal flexible solutions. For example, an employee refuses to attend evening meetings, which frustrates their supervisor.

Taylor: "I've had it with these evening meetings. I refuse to attend."

Sam: "Taylor, you know they're necessary. If you don't attend, there will be consequences."

Mediator: "Taylor, why won't you attend?" (*Why not?*)

Taylor: "It's unsafe at night in the parking lot."

Mediator: "So it's a safety concern?"

Taylor: "Yes, but also a family issue. I have kids, and my husband works nights. Finding childcare is difficult."

Mediator: "So you need to be home for your family."

Taylor: "Exactly."

Sam is surprised by the safety concern.

Sam: "I didn't know that. We can set up a buddy system and notify security."

Taylor: "That helps, but the meetings still disrupt my life."

Sam: "You knew this was part of the job."

Taylor: "Not at this frequency. It was once a month; now it's weekly or more. I think you're just disorganized."

Sam: "I'm not—I'm just overwhelmed."

The mediator shifts focus.

Mediator: "Sam, has the frequency of meetings increased?"

Sam: "Yes, but they're necessary."

Taylor: "Others feel the same way I do, if you asked them."

Mediator: "Can we adjust the schedule?"

Sixth Practice: Bring Transformative Power

Sam: [Pauses] "Maybe we try semi-monthly and check with the team for better times. Could occasional lunch meetings work?"

After discussion, they agree to fewer evening meetings, with safety measures in place. This scenario illustrates how rigid positions ("no more evening meetings") soften when interests are acknowledged, leading to practical solutions that start with an issue statement. Well-framed issue statements connect storytelling with problem-solving. Consider the underlying interests: for the employee, it's about safety and personal time; for the supervisor, it's about completing important work outside busy hours. Hearing these concerns, the mediator might frame a statement as follows: "How can we manage the timing and frequency of team meetings so that Taylor doesn't feel unsafe going out to the parking lot at night and has more time with family and Sam's concerns about fulfilling increasing work demands are satisfied?"

Conflicts often involve multiple issues, with some less tangible but equally important. In this particular case, the employee is concerned about the supervisor's management style, and the supervisor feels that the employee failed to communicate concerns sooner. The mediator uncovers additional issues, such as the employee's view of the supervisor as disorganized and unapproachable, while the supervisor feels unable to respond without being informed of issues.

The mediator might frame the statement like this: "We have these agenda items to discuss: employee's concern about approaching the supervisor during busy times for personal matters; supervisor's frustration about not being informed earlier; and finding time to address day-to-day issues. Does this sound right, or would you phrase it differently?"

The structure and wording of these statements vary because there are many ways to frame issues. The key measure of success is whether participants agree that the framing reflects the issue accurately, with room for clarification if needed. Let's look at a few more examples and then identify a few parameters to ensure well-framed statements.

Using "How do we…" or "How can we…" statements effectively captures participants' perspectives:

- **Teacher raises.** "How can the school fairly compensate teachers within budget constraints?"
- **Neighbor dispute.** "How can the noise issue be resolved so Mr. Smith can sleep and Mr. Jones avoids police visits?"
- **Coworker dispute.** "How can Joelle complete spreadsheets without interference while Caitlin gets timely reports?"

These statements acknowledge both sides' concerns neutrally, fostering mutual understanding. When broader collaboration is needed, a general statement works:

- "What can Joelle and Caitlin do to improve their working relationship?"
- "What can Taylor and Sam do to communicate better during busy periods?"

Visual Aids for Clarity

A simple chart highlights individual and shared interests:

Sixth Practice: Bring Transformative Power

Roberta	Randi	Both
Team cohesiveness	Business purpose for interaction	Successful events
Event planning info	Respect for time/ efficiency	Effective communication

This helps participants see shared goals beyond their differences.

Guidelines for Framing Statements[14]

- **One issue at a time** (e.g., focus only on evening meetings)
- **Neutral phrasing** (avoid bias or emotional language)
- **Mutual concerns only** (exclude issues that one party can't resolve)
- **Future focused** ("How can we..." instead of "Why did you...")

Clear framing shifts focus from problems to solutions, helping participants bridge gaps and move forward toward negotiation.

Negotiate by Exploring, Testing, and Analyzing Options for Resolution

Though breakthrough may occur rather quickly, many situations are more protracted, requiring a more deliberate application of standard negotiation practices to help participants address and overcome their resistance. Your job is to move participants through these practices as efficiently as possible. Anyone familiar with *Getting to Yes*, the classic text on interest-based negotiation, and other texts from the Harvard Negotiation Project will recognize these practices.[15]

They involve inquiry, testing, and analysis of options for resolution.

Encourage Idea Generation Before Evaluation
Encourage participants to brainstorm freely, sharing all possible solutions without judgment. Remind them that even unconventional ideas can spark creative solutions. Set the tone by saying, "Let's gather all possible solutions before evaluating them. Please share your ideas openly—there are no bad ideas at this stage. We'll assess them later. Who'd like to start?"

Resist early critiques, as they can stifle creativity and lead to unproductive conflict. If someone starts analyzing too soon, gently redirect: "Peter, we'll evaluate ideas soon. Right now, let's focus on gathering as many as possible."

If participants criticize each other's ideas, remind them, "Nancy, let's focus on solving the problem, not critiquing each other. We'll review ideas later."

Brainstorming duration depends on the complexity of the issue and participants' openness. It may be quick for simple issues or agreeable participants but longer for complex matters or when there's a need to address distractions. Guide the process to stay productive and move forward when needed.

Use Objective Criteria to Evaluate Options
After brainstorming, assess ideas using fairness and relevant standards, such as policies, market comparisons, or past agreements. Examples include the Kelley Blue Book, which helps value a used car, and salary data to help determine whether a job offer is reasonable based on qualifications and experience. You must inquire about the fairness and reasonableness of the options proposed against these standards. For example:

- **Employee-grievance issue involving employee request to reduce or eliminate discipline.** "Does a first act of what you are calling 'horse play' fall within the category of written warnings or oral warnings? How does the discipline policy interpret 'horse play'?"
- **Contract dispute regarding services for replacing a roof.** "How do you justify your insistence on the price stated in the contract, which is based on higher-grade shingles rather than the lower-grade shingles you ended up installing?"

For interpersonal conflicts, encourage setting mutually agreed-upon norms:

- **Two neighbors argue about maintaining a common fence line.** "Marcus says it should be okay to allow his dogs to relieve themselves along the fence and not have to scoop up their mess. It's fertilizer. Sylvester disagrees. Marcus feels Sylvester is negligent in keeping his side of the fence cleared of brush. Sylvester thinks once a year is sufficient. Can we agree on a standard for what maintaining the fence line means?"
- **Cubicle space.** "Laura, you feel that it is okay for your buddies to visit, as long as you keep conversation to a whisper. You and Barbara both agree on the need to keep noise down in the area. Have you discussed what 'noise' means and whether whispers constitute 'noise'?"

Refining Options for Agreement

After filtering out impractical ideas, focus on viable solutions. For example, in a contract dispute, rather than insisting on a full refund or complete retraction of complaints, parties might agree to:

- adjust pricing for unmet expectations,
- extend a warranty beyond the standard period, or
- amend an online review to acknowledge corrective efforts.

In workplace conflicts, instead of banning food or restricting communication, colleagues might:

- schedule visits and lunch breaks to minimize disruption,
- establish mutual respect for workspace preferences, and/or
- use meeting spaces for longer discussions.

Evaluating options often requires considering the interests of others to whom participants are accountable. By refining solutions collaboratively, participants create balanced, realistic agreements that address mutual interests.

Help Participants Find Options for a Tentative Agreement
For each issue, state your understanding of tentative agreements. Emphasize their tentative nature, as ultimate acceptance will depend on resolution of all issues in a final agreement.

- **Example 1:** "So, if I'm hearing you correctly, Joe, you may be willing to go along with accepting the lower-grade shingles so you don't have to deal with the hassle of redoing the whole project. Margie, you also agree that redoing the project would seriously inconvenience Roofs-R-Us, so you may agree to

Sixth Practice: Bring Transformative Power

an adjustment to the remainder that Joe owes to account not only for the true cost of the lower-grade shingles but for reasonable compensation for Joe's acceptance of the 30-year warranty vs. the 50-year warranty guaranteed on the higher-price shingles."
- **Example 2:** "Let me be sure I understand what you both may be willing to accept. Laura, you'll talk with your friends and request that they only visit briefly in the morning to check in and chitchat, and only briefly before you go off to lunch. These need not be whispers, but conversation should be limited to 10 minutes before you get back to work. Any longer discussions will only be had if they have a clear work purpose. For these discussions, you'll try to reserve a conference room. However, Barbara, you understand that longer work-related conversations in Laura's cubicle may be necessary if finding an alternative space is not feasible."

Test for Agreement and Explore Consequences

When a participant hesitates on an agreement, ask them to consider the consequences of not agreeing. Is it a deal-breaker, or can time help resolve it?

Example 1

- **Contractor reservation:** "Margie, Joe now seems prepared to let go of all other issues, provided the overall price reflects the lower-grade shingles and compensation for accepting a lesser manufacturer's warranty. I realize that the reduction in payment due is significant. But isn't the alternative complete

replacement? You both agree that step is hugely inconvenient. Is that what you want?"
- **Homeowner reservation:** "Joe, you said that you are likely to move sometime in the next three years. The warranty on the shingles is transferable to the new homeowner. Given the significant price reduction, how important is redoing the project and installing the 50-year shingles? Can it be justified given what you stand to realize with this agreement?"
- **To both:** "How will the judge see it? Isn't the decision either going to be to replace the roof entirely and Joe pays the full amount or to adjust the price with no replacement but Roofs-R-Us will not be compelled to make any guarantees either? Can't we agree that either option goes against the serious inconvenience you both want to avoid?"

Example 2

- **Barbara's reservation:** "Barbara, is complete quiet in the cubicle space realistic? Without these defined parameters that Laura is agreeing to—in other words, without a clear definition of 'noise'—won't it be difficult for you to raise a complaint later?"
- **Laura's reservation:** "Laura, can you justify random visits and conversation with coworkers that aren't work related? Yes, this agreement limits the amount of visiting and personal conversations you can have, but it doesn't rule them out. Isn't that better than Barbara continuing to raise concerns?"
- **To both:** "How will your supervisor feel if you don't find a workable solution? If you think this agreement

isn't ideal—perhaps no agreement is—is it not at least better than what your supervisor may insist upon?"

The practice of testing and exploring reservation points helps participants reflect in order to feel comfortable moving forward.

Record Tentative Agreements, Celebrate, and Move On to the Next Issue
This process will help participants reach tentative agreement for each issue in dispute. Many conflicts involve multiple issues, so it is important to acknowledge, preserve, and celebrate the tentative agreement reached on a single issue before going through the same process for the remaining issues.

- **Example 1:** "Okay, great, I've written down your tentative agreement regarding the lower-grade shingles. We've made great progress, and I want to commend you for your efforts. We still have a few issues to go over. Why don't we discuss the gutters next? What options do we have for addressing that issue?"
- **Example 2:** "Barbara and Laura, thank you for working together to find a resolution on the noise issue. I really appreciate your efforts to find common ground. I'm confident we'll find a solution to the remaining issues as well. Perhaps we could look at Laura's concerns about unpleasant smells coming from Barbara's cubicle. What options can we look at to address this concern?"

Support Participants' Legitimate Struggle with Impasse
During mediation, impasse may occur when participants feel that their needs haven't been met and doubt that resolution is possible. This is often due to unmet interests rather than bad-faith bargaining. Impasse can test patience, but it's also a moment for breakthrough, when genuine conversation about needs can lead to lasting agreements.

To navigate impasse, focus on specific reservations expressed, whether verbal or nonverbal, and dig deeper by asking such questions as "Why?" or "Why not?" This helps uncover underlying interests and allows for resolution.

- **Example 1 | Reason for impasse: Unmet needs or interests**

    - **Situation:** After a protracted conversation between two coworkers about how to work together without "getting in each other's way," one coworker expresses dissatisfaction, feeling that the process has become "mechanical" and misses the camaraderie they had before.
    - **Response:** Ask what might be missing, focusing on both tangible and intangible needs. "Jerri, it seems we haven't explored the impact this agreement will have on your long-term working relationship. Can you share more?"

- **Example 2 | Reason for impasse: Undefined problem**

    - **Situation:** Managers argue about management theories instead of how their teams can collaborate effectively. One manager focuses on operational procedures instead of co-leadership principles.

- **Response:** Revisit the purpose. "Mansi and Jamie, do we need to agree on management theory right now, or should we focus on concrete steps to improve team collaboration?"

- **Example 3 | Reason for impasse: Stuck on proposals**

  - **Situation:** Neighbors Marcus and Sylvester disagree on fence maintenance. Marcus wants Sylvester to clear his side monthly to prevent blockage of sunlight to his plants. Sylvester thinks once a year is enough and also wants Marcus to clean up after his dogs.
  - **Response:** Help them shift from narrow, self-serving solutions to broader goals. "Marcus and Sylvester, focusing only on proposals that benefit your interests may prevent you from improving your relationship. Can we think beyond your concerns to find solutions that meet both your needs?"

The above examples merely scratch the surface of the reasons for impasse. There are many others, including the following:

- Not taking responsibility for a proposed agreement
- Proposed agreement is not considered reasonable or achievable
- Participants feel overwhelmed, fearful, or worried
- There is concern over the objectivity of the mediator

Push and Pull Participants as Needed to Encourage Full Ownership and Breakthrough

As you guide participants toward breakthrough and resolution, continue using the skills and techniques discussed. Ensure that they take full ownership of the solution, addressing any tendency to shift responsibility to you or the other participant.

"Push" When Participants Need to Take Greater Responsibility

Use the tools from the Fourth Practice in chapter 5, "Sit with Others," to shift participants from unproductive conflict behaviors to collaborative ones. Confront passive (flight) or aggressive (fight) behaviors compassionately, helping participants to take ownership of the conflict and to advocate for themselves. Accordingly:

Confront with Firmness When Behaviors Are More Aggressive

- "Ani, you've spent the last few minutes telling Millie all the things she's done to create this problem. She acknowledged some of these issues previously. How is continuing to place blame helpful in this situation? Perhaps it's time to move to solutions."

Confront with Encouragement When Behaviors Are More Passive

- "Millie, I know Ani's accusations aren't sitting well with you. She's taken considerable time sharing them. I know you have your own perspectives and want them to be understood. I think it's time we work through them one by one so Ani can hear them. I've taken notes. Let's start with…"

Decide When and Where to Confront

These examples can be shared with both participants or separately, depending on the situation. Consider the need to control dynamics and avoid embarrassing a participant or violating their confidence. Use your best judgment, keeping in mind the impact on the mediation process. For example:

In a pre-mediation meeting, when observing up front that a participant tends to talk at length about their concerns while demonstrating little ability to reflect on the other participant's concerns. Acknowledge concerns and emotions and encourage them to consider a different tone in mediation so the other participant can truly hear them and not become reactive. Suggest that the best way to have their concerns understood is to sincerely listen to and seek to understand the other participant's concerns.

During mediation, when behavior has become or is becoming belligerent. Remind the offending participant of the ground rules, request that they immediately desist, and perhaps suggest that continued disrespect may result in the mediation being ended. (The greater the belligerence, the greater the need for directness over subtlety.)

In a separate meeting, when sensing that a participant has gone quiet because of subtle comments and behaviors exhibited by the other participant that are unclear to you as the mediator. Note what you are observing and ask the participant if there is something about the other participant that is making them uncomfortable and reticent to speak. Ask how you can help them address their concerns with the other participant.

"Pull" When Participants Must Decide for Themselves

At times, participants may look to you for answers when they're stuck, unaware that you might be just as unsure. These moments often require important decisions. You've covered everything, and now it's up to the participants to choose whether to move toward collaboration. It's not your job to decide for them. In these moments, where next steps aren't clear to anyone, becoming passive may be precisely what is needed to help participants reset and finally get serious about working matters out. Provide this reset by not suggesting anything or allowing the participants to force you into suggesting anything.

Sit Back, Do Nothing, and Rely on Spontaneity

It might seem like you're not doing much, but if participants constantly rely on you and look to you for answers, it could mean you've done too much already. You might have filled the silence, asked questions, or listened empathically because they weren't doing it themselves. Sometimes, however, there's nothing more you can do to help them communicate and decide.

By staying present and offering nonverbal cues that you're not going to be providing answers, participants may realize that the next move is theirs. Silence, waiting, and spontaneity can drive the process forward. When the moment arises, you can reenter to build on their progress and guide them toward a breakthrough.

Suggest a Break and Give Participants Something to Think About and Respond to Upon Their Return

This surprisingly successful strategy works well after participants have exhausted their stories and arguments. I often suggest a break after I've framed the issues into problem statements. This allows them to reset, think about

Sixth Practice: Bring Transformative Power

the problems over break, and begin to solve them upon their return.

Trust your intuition when suggesting a break. Sometimes I just give a return time, but other times I ask participants to reflect on specific questions, acknowledge the other person's perspective, and consider their own role in the conflict. What I ask depends on the stage of mediation, as guiding them toward self-reflection too early can lead to resistance.

This simple reset often helps us move forward more constructively. It provides a breather, reducing tension and allowing for clearer focus on solutions. It also subtly highlights the gravity of the situation, pushing participants to realize the need for resolution. The break also gives the mediator time to process and synthesize each participant's story, framing the issues in a way that encourages solution-building. Don't underestimate the power of a reset to refresh the process and allow you and the participants to refocus and find clarity where it had been absent moments before.

Say "I Don't Know" and that It's Not Your Job, but Rather Theirs, to Know

This strategy involves being up front about your thoughts and feelings, acknowledging that you don't have a quick solution. You may need to remind participants that it's time to shift from sharing perspectives to identifying solutions. Though you've been guiding the process, the focus must now be on their decisions, not further discussion. By being clear, you signal that they can no longer depend solely on you and must take responsibility for moving forward. This is an important shift as it mirrors what the reality of their relationship will be after mediation ends.

Look for and Exploit Moments for Breakthrough to Occur
There's no simple answer to what triggers a breakthrough or when it will happen. Breakthrough requires a catalyst that shifts the conversation from argument to problem-solving. This catalyst can be obvious or subtle, often a change in perspective, behavior, or reaction that opens the door to resolution. The skills in this section help participants clarify potential solutions. A well-framed issue statement shifts perspectives, moving beyond self-centered views and highlighting concerns, guiding them toward a path forward.

Solutions come more readily after breakthrough. The short list that follows (with examples) identifies additional situations where breakthrough can occur and provide opportunities for reaching resolution.

- **Exhaustion.** Participants don't always expect mediation to be intense or time-consuming, but exhaustion can lead to concessions or breakthroughs. Though you shouldn't exploit fatigue to force a resolution, doing so can help lower defenses, allowing the individuals to recognize their role in the problem and how to resolve it.
- **A small conciliatory gesture is reciprocated.** Many entering mediation are naturally conciliatory, seeking fairness and resolution. A participant may acknowledge their role, prompting the other to reciprocate, such as saying, "I could have responded differently too. I didn't have to be so angry."
- **Letting go of less-important issues creates a pathway to resolving more-important issues.** Two employees argue over weekly meeting times, with one of them insisting on a fixed schedule. But once they accept the impracticality of such a schedule, they

Sixth Practice: Bring Transformative Power

shift focus to deeper concerns about communication styles and meeting productivity.
- **New information changes perspective.** A manager reluctantly agrees to mediation for two team members. As they uncover a series of interactions with the boss, it becomes clear that he has fueled the conflict with misinformation. This revelation paves the way to restore trust and address the true issue.
- **Facing imminent loss prompts change.** A mediation to dissolve a business partnership shifts toward exploring reconciliation. One partner, distrusting the other's mood swings and lack of focus, suspects that personal struggles are clouding business. The mediator helps clarify what must be done in order to restore trust. In tears, the partner expresses remorse, leading to a discussion about seeking counseling, setting conditions, and establishing a timeline before deciding on the partnership's future.
- **Willingness to be vulnerable.** Participants are often reluctant to be vulnerable, but when they are, expressions of regret and intent to repair relationships can drive resolution. This can't be forced, but mediation provides a safe space where such outcomes are possible, as long as participants feel that their vulnerability won't be exploited.

Facilitating Breakthrough Moments in Mediation

Despite our best efforts, sometimes mediation can stall. Participants struggle to find common ground, see no room for agreement, and may feel like giving up. Yet it is often in these darkest moments that breakthroughs occur.

Breakthrough in mediation isn't just about resolution but also overcoming limiting behaviors to achieve clarity.

Remember our example from earlier in the chapter. Stacy provided Annalise with a safe space to express her concerns and offered Lexi the same opportunity. She patiently ensured balance, checking in with Lexi even after she'd disengaged from the conversation.

Stacy helped Annalise move past politeness to express her true needs and challenged Lexi to reflect on her lack of engagement. She framed their differing perspectives and guided them toward defining their walk-away points. Stacy approached this with caution, recognizing the shift toward accountability in workplace culture.

Though participants ultimately decide when and how resolution happens, mediators play a powerful role in facilitating these moments. There is no single skill or technique that guarantees a breakthrough, but the tools discussed in this book can help create the right conditions. More importantly, breakthrough depends on patience, persistence, and the ability to guide participants toward a shift in perspective.

Keys to Guiding Breakthrough

1. **Develop a sense of sacredness in your role.** Mediation is an honor and a privilege. Participants trust you to help transform their relationships and bring positive change. If you lack this sense of purpose, your energy and enthusiasm may wane when participants need you most. Stay mindful of what's at stake and fully engage in the process.
2. **Model patience and commitment.** Encourage participants to take their time—schedule extended sessions, turn off distractions, and avoid rushing. Lead by example. If you show signs of impatience or exhaustion, they will pick up on it. Set aside urgency for outside matters and remain calm, present, and patient.

3. Double down on your effort. The mediation process is much harder for participants than for you. Their emotional investment can make them want to give up prematurely. Recognize this and commit twice as much effort to helping them stay engaged. Resist the temptation—yours and theirs—to quit before true resolution is possible.

4. Recognize your power. As a mediator, your words, body language, and demeanor can either move the process forward or shut it down. A careless comment or moment of doubt can halt progress just as participants are on the verge of a breakthrough. Conversely, your confidence, calm, and encouragement can shift their perspective and open new possibilities. Be intentional with your influence.

Breakthrough moments signal that resolution may be imminent. We can't guarantee that our efforts will always lead to a breakthrough, as achieving such a result is up to the participants, but we can set the stage for breakthrough to occur by facilitating processes that will guide them there. When you are almost there and it is time to capture their agreement, ensure that they make concrete commitments for fulfilling its terms and support a positive conclusion. Your challenge is to be vigilant in your effort to reach these moments in order to capitalize on them. When you do, you can help support a dignified exit.

Chapter 7 Reflective Exercise

Prepare for Breakthrough Opportunities

The following template presents a tool for capturing participants' respective positions and interests, framing issues, identifying possible options for resolution and potential barriers, and recording tentative agreements.

Instructions for Using the Mediation Template

1. **Preparation Before Mediation:**
    - After meeting with the participants, use this tool to capture your initial thoughts and impressions.
    - Record the participants' positions, interests, issues, and potential solutions.
    - Keep in mind that these notes are preliminary and should not be considered final until the mediation takes place.
2. **During Mediation:**
    - Use the template throughout the mediation process to track the evolution of the conversation.
    - Update it with new insights, options for resolution, and any tentative agreements as the mediation unfolds.
3. **Identify Key Areas:**
    - **Positions and interests.** Capture each participant's stance and underlying interests.
    - **Issues.** Frame the key points of conflict clearly.
    - **Options for resolution.** List possible solutions that arise.

Sixth Practice: Bring Transformative Power

- ○ **Barriers.** Identify any challenges or concerns that may hinder resolution.
- ○ **Tentative agreements.** Record agreements that participants discuss, keeping them flexible until final resolution.
4. **Post-Mediation:**
    - ○ Review and refine the notes as the participants work toward breakthrough moments.
    - ○ Adapt the tool as needed to continue facilitating progress.
5. **Final Agreement:**
    - ○ Once a breakthrough is reached, use the template to help formalize the final agreement.

For an example based on Stacy's mediation with Annalise and Lexi, please see the resources section at the end of the book.

Preparing for Breakthrough
Participant A:
Participant B:
Conflict Situation:
Positions: What are the hard-and-fast, "yes or no" positions that each participant is holding onto?
Why is each position so important to the participant?
Why are alternatives to this position **not** possible?

Participant A:	Participant B:

Interests: What interests (issues, needs, concerns, values, etc.) do you perceive are important to each participant that lie beneath the positions they are taking?

Think in terms of interests that, if met, would help participants move from hard-and-fast, "yes or no" positions to possibilities for finding common ground with each other.

Participant A:	Participant B:

Framing Statement: Considering their varying interests, how would you frame the issues in a compelling way that provides a basis for helping the participants attempt to resolve the matter?

Issue 1:

Issue 2:

Issue 3:

(add additional issues as needed)

Options and Alternatives for Resolution: What options have the participants suggested, or might they consider, to resolve each issue you've identified (as captured in your framing statement)?

How will these options be evaluated? What criteria will be used?

Which options are more viable than others?

Participant A:	Participant B:

Impasse: What resistance is each participant expressing (verbally or implicitly) that may prevent them from accepting an option or proposal?

What tools, strategies, and/or approaches might you utilize to help the participant overcome this resistance? (Note: if resistance is deeper than a legitimate struggle with impasse, such as lack of good faith, consider the strategies covered in the next chapter, "Support a Dignified Exit.")

Participant A:	Participant B:

Agreements: What tentative agreements are possible to resolve the issues you've identified (as captured in the framing statement)? (Note: keep track of these for developing the final agreement.)

(add additional items as needed)

Notes: Use this space to make notes about other aspects of the conflict that may help you in mediating. In particular, consider possible moments and opportunities that might occur for which you can "push" or "pull" participants toward breakthrough.

Chapter 8

Seventh Practice: Support a Dignified Exit

Conclude with Grace, Dignity, and Respect, No Matter the Outcome

"We've arrived. Watch your step and travel safely."

Chapter Goals

By the end of this chapter, you will:

- embrace working tirelessly to help participants overcome legitimate resistance,
- be ready to capture and record agreements and celebrate, and
- understand how to support participants as they leave mediation, regardless of outcome.

We've reached the last stop on *The Mediation Road Map*; it's time for the participants to exit the bus. During the bumpy ride, our role was to facilitate transformation, but the outcome—resolution, no resolution, or an unresolved middle ground—is ultimately up to the participants. Everyday mediators accept that the outcome is always within the participants' power to grasp. Even if participants leave dissatisfied, they gain clarity on the root causes of their conflict and may be better equipped to resolve it later. Regardless of the result, it's important to validate their efforts and help them maintain dignity, providing the support and tools needed to move forward confidently.

A Story: "Support a Dignified Exit" in Action

Sumiko recently graduated with a degree in peace and conflict studies and a business minor. She met Sam, an attorney, at a networking event, who suggested she contact Maggie, who was starting a nonprofit focused on community peacebuilding.

Maggie, whose main job was as director of community engagement at a truck-engine company, shared her passion for the nonprofit. "I've found some good partners," she said, "and I plan to go full-time once we've incorporated, formed a board, and secured some funding for operating expenses and a modest salary for myself."

By the end of the meeting, Maggie asked Sumiko if she would help develop the nonprofit and serve on the board. She had recruited three others, including Sam, but still needed a secretary. Sumiko jumped in and they got busy. It quickly became evident how much Maggie needed an assistant. She was great at big ideas and effective at connecting with others, but finer details escaped her. Sumiko also worked with Sam to develop and file the incorporation documents, which was when she first learned that Maggie and Sam's relationship was strained.

"That's Maggie," Sam said, "always galloping ahead, leaving the rest of us to eat her dust."

The board formed with Sumiko as secretary, Maggie as unpaid director, and Sam as chair, providing legal counsel. Chrystal, vice chair, was well connected in African-American and Latino communities, ran a litigation and mediation practice, and taught mediation at the law school. She would rally community support and recruit volunteer mediators. She recommended Maxwell, a well-connected bank VP, as treasurer.

Over three months, Maggie secured small grants for initial expenses, and she and Chrystal built awareness among community leaders who would train as mediators. Sumiko, with a marketing firm's help, developed a website and social media presence. Board members leveraged their networks to explore funding, partnerships, and potential service users, including corporate donors, government agencies, and legal professionals.

Sumiko was excited to be part of the launch and found Maggie's relentless drive inspiring but also overwhelming. Board meetings became a tug-of-war between Maggie's ambition and Sam's caution. This balance held—until the fourth meeting, when tensions came to a head.

"I think we're ready to launch," said Maggie.

"I don't know," replied Sam. "There are still a lot of details that don't quite seem in place."

"Well, I think we're ready, and here's why."

Maggie delivered a passionate but scattered speech, acknowledging limited funds, a lower-than-planned salary for her, and only a tentative offer for office space. Despite this, she urged action, warning that delays could stall momentum and deter supporters.

"Once again, I'll say that the numbers still don't add up, Maggie," Sam insisted.

Sam and Maxwell again reviewed the budget with her. As they did so, Maggie interrupted with arguments, starting with "Yes, but what about…" and "I think you're missing the larger point that…"

This argument continued for a half hour. Chrystal occasionally suggested that they each give consideration to the other's point.

Finally, exasperated, Maggie exclaimed, "Sam, stop. You're crushing dreams!"

"Crushing dreams? Whose dreams? Is that what this is about? Your vanity?"

"That's not fair," Maggie countered. "You know I meant the nonprofit."

"Well, as long as I'm chair, I need to think about what's best for the organization."

"I know, but you're being too cautious. If we aren't careful, we'll lose all that we've built."

"We'll lose it anyway. Careful is exactly what I'm being."

"But if you could only consider what I'm saying. What about…"

"That's enough. I said no."

The room went quiet. After a moment, Maggie said, visibly angry, "No?!? What do you mean 'no'? We may have our disagreements, but you've never said no."

"Well, all I have to say is do you want my help or not? I don't have to do this, you know. Of course, the firm will pull out as well. But you'll still have your dream. Go for it."

"Hey, Maggie, Sam," interrupted Chrystal, "Before we say anything more that we might regret, I propose we adjourn for the evening and reconvene in two weeks."

Two weeks passed with no progress. Maggie tried reaching Sam, but he was unavailable. Frustrated, she sent a long, emotional email to the board. Sam replied vaguely, hinting at resignation. Maggie sent another impassioned email, which Sam ignored. The board was left in limbo. Sumiko tried engaging Maggie, but she gave little feedback. Sumiko then reached out to Chrystal for advice. "I don't know what to do," Sumiko said. "This goes against Maggie's vision."

"Does that surprise you?" Chrystal asked.

Sumiko paused. "No, but I thought we had something."

Seventh Practice: Support a Dignified Exit

"We still do. Don't you believe that?"

"Yes. But if we can't come together, Maggie's right: we'll lose momentum."

Chrystal remained calm, offering wisdom from experience. She shared her background, gave Sumiko advice about law school, and reminded her not to pin all her hopes on one outcome. Sumiko asked if Chrystal would mediate. Noticing something special in Sumiko, Chrystal suggested that she would do a better job. Sumiko protested—she had no experience. Chrystal wasn't convinced.

That night, while working her part-time job, Sumiko remembered unfinished paperwork she had to do for the nonprofit. The next morning, she emailed a meeting request to complete the filings, a test to see if Sam would show. He did, making small talk with Maggie, but before Sumiko could pull out the documents, Sam balked, "I came here because I thought it best to meet in person. I don't think I'm what you need. That was evident from the last meeting. Chrystal, I propose you step in as chair."

"Sorry, Sam, I'm already overcommitted," replied Chrystal. "I think you are what we need."

Maggie sighed. "It's alright, Sam. I've been thinking. Thank you for your work. I know you don't support this anymore. I need to regroup. We've lost time, but I'll find a way."

"It's not that I don't support you," said Sam.

"I'm not so sure. But it's okay."

Sam hesitated, then nodded. "Alright, I guess that's it. I'll be going."

He stood up as Maggie quietly gathered her papers.

"No," came a voice, softly. It took a moment to realize the voice was Sumiko's.

"What?" asked Sam.

"I said 'no.' You're not the only one who can say it. I think you need to stay a bit longer."

"I don't know what that's going to accomplish."
"You need to stay."
"Agreed," added Chrystal.
"Yes, agreed," Maxwell confirmed.

Sam sat back down.

Sumiko surprised herself when she spoke up and was now unsure where to begin. "I know I don't say a lot at these meetings," she began, tentatively. "I'm just trying to keep up. I really appreciate this opportunity and am excited about it. And I appreciate learning from all of you. Maggie and Sam, you've both got so much to offer, and it's a shame if things end this way. But I have to tell you that working between you two can be so frustrating. It's no wonder we are where we are."

Sumiko took a moment and then added, "Here's what I'm seeing."

She noted how Sam and Maggie often talked over each other. Maggie's passion was refreshing but made it hard for her to pause and absorb others' input. Maybe she felt the need to constantly persuade, not realizing that they shared her vision—they just expressed it differently. A little more calmness and reflection might help. As if on cue, Maggie sat forward and said, "Sumiko, you don't understand. Sam is trying to—"

"Maggie," Chrystal interrupted. "I think you've just made Sumiko's point."

"We really are on board with you," added Sumiko, who then shared how difficult it was to see Sam so reactive to Maggie's energy and elevated expressions of emotion.

It was also difficult to see Sam engage in innuendo and sarcasm, often out of Maggie's earshot, though he also couldn't resist a "zinger" now and then in her presence. Perhaps his venting was his way of coping with Maggie's relentless advocacy.

Seventh Practice: Support a Dignified Exit

"We need a way to communicate our concerns with one another honestly. I understand how Maggie can react, but you're escalating it."

Sam also pushed back, suggesting that Maggie couldn't—or perhaps wouldn't—be contained, and it would ultimately be both her downfall and the nonprofit's. He couldn't support that.

Maggie interjected, "Well, I think you also—"

Chrystal held up her hand. "That's what we're here to figure out, but I hear Sumiko saying it starts with you two. Well, actually, all of us. Is that it, Sumiko?"

"Yeah, I don't see how we can proceed otherwise."

It was a late night, with everyone calling family and babysitters. With Chrystal's help, Sumiko encouraged open dialogue about their interactions and impact. Chrystal, Maxwell, and Sumiko shared their own contributions to the challenges. As Sumiko began to ask Sam about staying on the board, Chrystal intervened. "It's too early for that. We need to sleep on it."

They agreed to limit contact until the following week's meeting, where Sam's presence—or absence—would determine the next steps. Regardless, Chrystal emphasized that Maggie shouldn't see Sam as an enemy and that both should reflect on what mattered to each other and the board. Even if Sam resigned, a future coffee meeting with Maggie wouldn't be a bad idea.

Outside, Chrystal praised Sumiko's courage. Sumiko admitted her rookie mistake and said that she thought they needed a decision. Chrystal told her that would have forced the issue and sometimes it's okay to leave things unclear.

Earning Your Keep as an Everyday Mediator

When mediation appears no closer to resolution than before it began, perhaps the participants haven't found an opportunity to let down their guard. Though you have encouraged them to listen and reflect on each other's concerns, they simply aren't accustomed to a process in which giving deference and attempting to meet one another's needs is expected. It's time to take a deep breath. They must go to their neutral corners, reflect, and seriously evaluate what is so important that it is worth continuing the fight. And you must allow them to do so.

Consider Sumiko from this story. She displayed the traits of a novice mediator: earnestness, tentativeness, a desire to get it right, and some impatience for resolution. This isn't a flaw; it's just the reality of sincerely wanting to help. She grappled with doubt—both in the conflict's resolution and in herself as the mediator. We all face such doubts and may hesitate to step into conflicts.

Yet Sumiko showed courage. She didn't know when or how the opportunity for mediation would arise, but when it did, she seized it. In that moment, she relied not on textbooks but on instinct, transforming how Sam, Maggie, and the board interacted. Chrystal demonstrated the traits of an experienced mediator: calm, intuitive, and possessing a keen sense of when to push or allow for reflection. She had no expectation of a guaranteed outcome and refused to let Sumiko blame herself if resolution wasn't reached.

Both Chrystal and Sumiko respected the process. Sam and Maggie were stuck debating the launch, unable to move forward. Sumiko reframed their frustration, shifting focus from the issue itself to their communication. Chrystal reinforced this by allowing space rather than forcing a decision. Together, they upheld the dignity of all involved, recognizing that resolving relationships was key to making sound decisions for the nonprofit's future.

Address Ongoing Resistance

Maggie and Sam's resistance was clear. Resistance occurs when a participant refuses to continue mediation, signaling a desire to end negotiations. Unlike impasse, which may be resolved in order to allow mediation to continue, resistance often stems from a participant feeling that they've achieved their goals, hold more power, or don't value the relationship enough to continue. They may also have reached their walk-away point and are unwilling to concede more. If one participant is satisfied, mediation could end. If the other is not, you may attempt to address the resistance and continue. There are a number of resister beliefs to explore and address:

If resister believes:	Inquire:	Example:
The situation isn't as important or serious as the other participant believes.	Does the participant fully understand the consequences for discontinuing mediation?	Resister: The coworker believes that cooperating with their colleague isn't important: "She'll get me the reports I need; what choice does she have?" Through mediation, the resister's coworker asserts that, without cooperation, the resister will get the reports but not her expertise in explaining them, making her look foolish before constituents.

If resister believes:	Inquire:	Example:
Facts and narratives about the conflict justify her resistance.	Are any facts missed or narratives misinterpreted that might reasonably change the participant's perception?	Resister: The supervisor believes that their employee's reluctance to take on new assignments, such as making presentations at meetings, is simply her wanting things to be as "comfortable" as the way they were with her former supervisor. She may have to move to negative performance ratings. Through mediation, the employee reluctantly reveals that she has a social-phobia disorder that makes it difficult to speak before large groups. This provides the supervisor with a new understanding of how to work with her.

Seventh Practice: Support a Dignified Exit

If resister believes:	Inquire:	Example:
The relationship with the other participant isn't as important as that participant believes.	Are there unmet needs that the resister has not considered that depend on this relationship?	Resister: One friend believes that she does not need to change her behaviors, which the other friend feels reflects a consistent pattern of negativity and codependence. The resister also is an alcoholic. During mediation, the friend tearfully expresses her love for the resister but that she can no longer tolerate the treatment. If resister wants to continue as friends, she must evaluate her choices. Otherwise, the friend will withdraw her support.

If resister believes:	Inquire:	Example:
The communication process prevents further meaningful mediation.	What miscues or misunderstandings have occurred that led to that conclusion?	Resister: The employee believes that his supervisor is a bully and is gruff, insensitive, and overly direct. The employee appears to have a "hair trigger," reacting negatively to any perceived negative comment. The mediator talks through examples raised by the employee to address the supervisor's communication style point by point. The supervisor acknowledges the need to address certain aspects of their communication style but asserts the need to be "direct but fair" and based on problematic behaviors exhibited by the employee.

If resister believes:	Inquire:	Example:
Further negotiation is pointless.	Is the participant open to options presented or aware of consequences for discontinuing negotiations?	Resister: The roof contractor feels that all options presented so far in the dispute with the homeowner about faulty installation of shingles and gutters requires her to make deep concessions on price. It might simply be better to take her chances in small-claims court for payment still due. Through mediation, the homeowner signals his willingness to accept the lesser-grade shingles that the contractor mistakenly installed in exchange for a significant price reduction but feels confident that the contractor will be required to make a complete replacement if the matter proceeds to small-claims court. The contractor accepts the reality that it is better to accept a lesser payment than fight the matter further.

If resister believes:	Inquire:	Example:
The maximum possible has been achieved and no further concessions are possible.	Is the participant's assessment of the walk-away point based on valid, objective criteria?	In the same scenario, the resisting roof contractor feels that the 20% price reduction offered by the homeowner cuts deeper than the value and cost of the lesser shingles would warrant. The homeowner produces data showing the significantly inferior value of the lesser shingles compared with the shingles for which he contracted, justifying a 35% price reduction. He states, "I'm willing to pay more just to be done with the hassle. I'm moving in three years anyway."

Resistance often ties to participants' assessment of their walk-away points, also referred to as the "best alternative to a negotiated agreement" (BATNA), and how they weigh the costs of leaving versus staying. Does one participant have a stronger BATNA than initially realized? Gaining new information, taking into account unconsidered consequences, and/or evaluating positions against objective criteria can help address resistance and keep negotiations moving toward agreement.

Manage Hard-Bargainers and Their Expectations

Hard bargaining is a form of resistance wherein participants use win-lose tactics to press their advantage, often through personal attacks or aggressive posturing. Some use it as their only approach, whereas others may soften if/when options align with their interests. In mediation, assess the motivations behind hard bargaining and respond accordingly. Some responses include the following:

1. Educate participants about the mediation process and how it contrasts with adversarial bargaining. Mediation implies a collaborative process. No promises are made, but there is an expectation that participants will attempt to understand others' perspectives and explore possibilities for resolution. Participants have agreed to mediation. Hard bargaining doesn't fit this picture. Take time to ensure that the participants understand the purpose of mediation and how their behaviors aren't helpful, at least if they are sincere about wanting a resolution. For example:

> In an initial meeting prior to mediation, an employee in a dispute with a coworker says, "I'm going to make it really simple for Sam. Either he accepts the way I've laid things out for completing this project or I'm going over his head to talk to our boss. I'm the senior associate on this team, and I know what I'm talking about. Sam's going to need to get in line."

> Mediator response: "I know you're frustrated, but I think your supervisor has asked you to work this out through mediation in a collaborative manner. Mediation isn't a process for making take-it-or-leave-it demands. Rather, it's a process for

give-and-take. Do you think you can agree to that, or at least try?"

You may need to further explain how take-it-or-leave-it approaches may only create greater resistance in the other participant and won't ultimately benefit the hard-bargainer's interests either.

2. Convert hard-bargaining approaches to opportunities for solving problems. Hard bargaining is often characterized by aggressive posturing and demands that appear nonnegotiable, such as take-it-or-leave-it gambits, "exploding" offers that expire by an arbitrary deadline ("This offer is off the table after 5:00 p.m."), and last-minute demands during mediation that are far outside the bargaining range previously discussed. Calmly respond by using reason and logic, highlighting the challenges that their demands present and inviting their input in solving the dilemma they've posed. For example:

(Aggressive posturing)

> Cameron blusters on about the terrible injustice he's experienced at the hands of Karl, who he claims has damaged his reputation among their fraternity brothers. He demands at one point, "Karl needs to grovel for my forgiveness and go to our fraternity brothers in a formal meeting and retract all the lies he's told and apologize publicly. Nothing else will do." As Karl tries either to inquire about the alleged statements he's made that were damaging or provide an explanation for this actions, Cameron continues to bluster, pointing his finger and giving little opportunity to

Seventh Practice: Support a Dignified Exit

explore specific concerns or concrete information to support his claims.

Mediator response: "Cameron, I see that you feel a lot of hurt over this situation and have a clear picture of what you want. But it's not clear to me, and doesn't appear to be clear to Karl, what your specific hurts are. Raising your voice and finger-pointing don't help. Can we talk through your concerns in a calmer manner so Karl can have a chance to understand more deeply your concerns and why you feel so hurt? Perhaps we could look at a couple examples and walk through them step-by-step to see what's happened?"

(Nonnegotiable demand)

Cameron continues to insist on a public apology in a formal meeting with their fraternity brothers and that nothing short of that will do. If Karl can't agree, "Then there's nothing else to talk about," Cameron insists.

Mediator response: "Cameron, you've really narrowed down the options that Karl might consider to respond to your concerns. If that becomes the sticking point, with 'nothing else to talk about,' as you say, then Karl may have no incentive to continue the mediation either. I wonder how all the other concerns you have about Karl's behavior and your need for him to understand more deeply how you've been hurt will remain unaddressed. Is there really nothing to salvage here short of a public apology, or is it in your best interests to stay and consider whether there are other options that might help you address the hurt you feel?"

3. Don't tolerate personal attacks, particularly when directed at other participants. Personal attacks are likely part of the ground rules you have established. Calm yet firm reminders in response to initial attacks may need to escalate to more confrontational, yet still respectful, responses if the attacks continue. You must decide the appropriate forum for addressing these behaviors, whether in front of the other participant or in private. For example:

(Early in mediation)

Roberto: "Debbie is a judgmental fool."

Mediator: "Roberto, we agreed to watch our labels and insults. That's not helpful. Let's be mindful of such statements."

Roberto: "Okay. Sorry."

(Later in mediation)

Roberto: "Debbie, stop being such a prude. We all like to tell a joke every now and again to relieve stress. If you don't like it, join a convent."

Mediator: "Let me stop you there, Roberto. We talked about this. No insults and offensive labels. If we can't talk about this maturely, I'm not sure there is a point in continuing."

You may at times also be able to convert personal attacks, particularly if they are directed at you, into attacks on the problem. For example:

(Attack on mediator's attempt to frame the issues)

Participant: "You're defining the problem all wrong. You're skirting over a whole bunch of issues that need to be addressed."

Mediator response: "Great, please help me fill in the gaps. I want to be sure I cover all the issues to both your satisfaction."

(Attack on the mediator's understanding of details underlying the conflict)

Participant: "I don't think you've listened to a word I've said. That is not what happened at all. You've missed the key point of this whole situation."

Mediator response: "Okay, please fill me in. I want to be sure I haven't overlooked anything. The goal is clarity, and you can help us achieve that."

4. Name the game. There is an endless list of game-playing tactics that hard-bargainers use, including "dirty tricks," thinking they're being clever. You can counter this by calling out the tactic and making it clear that it won't work in the mediation setting. For example:

(Exploding demand)

Tamarah insists that Tyler accept her proposal now or she will not honor the agreement they've reached thus far and take action to protect her interests against Tyler, implying a lawsuit.

Mediator response: "Tamarah, I see that you're trying to make an arbitrary demand that Tyler accept your proposal today or the deal is off. Tyler has indicated that he needs to think about it. If we need to reconvene tomorrow to continue this discussion, I don't see why we couldn't do that. I don't see the urgency here. Nothing is going to change overnight that would require his immediate acceptance."

(Last-minute demand)

As the mediator summarizes the details of the agreement as part of the wrap-up, Thomas states, "You know, this just occurred to me. It's going to cost me at least $500 in storage rental and insurance to store my items from the garage while Jake does the repairs. I'm going to need that as part of this deal."

Mediator response: "Thomas, Jake has honored all your previous requests and agreed to increase the lump-sum payment he will make, now at $6,000, to address all the issues involving damage to your garage, plus the inconvenience. He is also doing the repairs himself. It's now almost 5:00 p.m. and you previously agreed to these terms. This seems like a last-minute add-on, which seemingly leaves Jake no alternative but to accept, lest the whole deal fall through. I'm not sure that honors the good-faith pledge you agreed to when we started this mediation."

Admonish Participants Who Were Never Serious
If efforts to address hard bargaining reveal no legitimate resistance, it may be time to end the mediation. This often signals that one or more participant was never truly interested in a collaborative outcome, perhaps using the process to gain insight, maintain power, or manipulate the situation.

Avoid getting drawn in. Be prepared to confront the participant, reminding them of your role and the mediation's purpose, which their behavior contradicts. Let them know that the mediation cannot proceed unless they cooperate, and in most cases, a separate meeting may be necessary before concluding the process.

Though most jurisdictions prohibit using mediation discussions in future litigation, organizational grievance hearings may not have such rules. Nevertheless, confidentiality should still be respected. Remind participants not to misuse the process, even if they aren't serious about resolving the conflict.

Navigate Unsettled Ground
It's rewarding when participants reach a positive outcome for everyone involved, leaving with hope and clear steps for resolution. However, many mediations fall into the middle ground, where only partial agreements are reached or there's no agreement at all, yet options such as lawsuits or quitting aren't viable. In these situations, help participants navigate this uncertain space as productively as possible.

Explore What Participants Must Do with No or Only Partial Agreement

Encourage participants to imagine life and their relationship should they not reach a satisfactory agreement. What will their world look like in that scenario? Use appreciative inquiry to prompt reflection. Revisit this question as a last attempt to explore if full agreement is still possible: "Please envision a world where you work well together. What does that look like? What do you experience when things are going well?" Allow time for reflection and responses.

This may lead to inquiries about what each needs to do in order to reach this ideal. Ask, "What do you need from the other person to achieve this?" and "What must you each commit to for this new reality to happen?" Though articulating what they need from each other is easier than identifying their own changes, the closing of mediation might be the push they need to focus on the changes they must make, not just those they expect from others.

Whether asking about life "with" or "without" an agreement, the point is to challenge them to soberly reflect on these questions before ending in an unsettled state.

> "I don't want to press if we really aren't going to get anywhere. But I would like you each to reflect on what this will really mean. Have you considered how (your relationship, working together, completing the project, continuing your dispute as neighbors, etc.) will occur without finding agreement? You still have to find a way to get along, right? What are you going to do?"

However you guide this inquiry, there are at least two additional lines of inquiry to explore. The first is the participants' responsibilities to absent third parties. For example, two disputing coworkers must consider how to explain their lack of agreement to their mutual boss:

> "What will Francine think when we tell her that you haven't reached an agreement? What do you think she'll do? What would you do in her situation?"

Or other interested parties:

> "How will your team members feel about this? Haven't they also been frustrated about this situation? Don't you owe something to them, or at least a reasonable explanation?"

> "Marcus and Sylvester, it appears that we've found no reasonable way to address how you'll maintain the fence between your yards. But aren't your wives just as frustrated as you are? What will you tell them? What will they expect?"

Second, when no lasting agreement is reached, participants must still consider behavioral expectations. A positive outcome often stems from deeper reflection and genuine commitments to change. Without such reflection, participants may lack the willingness to make meaningful commitments. However, with external pressures from supervisors, neighbors, or colleagues, they may modify their behavior in order to avoid negative consequences, even if the change feels mechanical and driven by self-preservation rather than a desire to improve the relationship. You might ask:

> "What must you each do so Francine doesn't take the next step, such as impose discipline?"

"What will your wives expect so that they don't have to hear your continued complaints about each other regarding the fence?"

"Mansi and Jamie, if your teams continue to see you disagree, are you concerned how this may further fuel their frustration? What are you going to do so this won't happen?"

"Laura, if you refuse to set your own boundaries regarding how frequently your friends visit your cubicle or for how long, what might you reasonably expect Barbara to do? Is it possible she'll complain all the more to your supervisor?"

Through such inquiry, participants may identify at least a few steps to keep the peace and avoid hot water for themselves.

Use Mediation to Educate

When training others on mediation, I introduce Bernard Mayer's concept of "conflict engagement" from his book *Beyond Neutrality: Confronting the Crisis in Conflict Resolution*.[16] In it, Mayer stated, "Engaging in conflict means accepting the challenges of a conflict, whatever its type or stage of development may be, with courage and wisdom without automatically assuming that resolution is an appropriate goal."[17] Success in mediation shouldn't always be defined by resolving a dispute but rather by how well participants engage with it. For example, in long-standing international conflicts, parties may remain at odds but still find ways to engage in more productive processes, achieving workable coexistence despite ongoing tension.

The mediation process from this perspective offers opportunities for learning more about each other, their interests, values, and preferred methods for communicating and interacting so that each can find ways to accommodate the other after mediation, even in the midst of continued contention. After a time, as they realize more positive outcomes by cooperating, even if begrudgingly, they may later achieve a more durable resolution.

Some participants may leave mediation feeling frustrated as it's often their first chance to truly be heard or understand the other's perspective. They're still too close to the hurt to offer concessions or solutions. Over time, however, they may process their emotions and gradually begin to cooperate, either through natural behavioral changes or by returning to mediation later on.

Believe that you are accomplishing something simply by providing a forum for disputing participants to talk through their differences, even if after they hear one another out, they walk away still upset and angry. Whether you—or they—realize it, you are educating them on how to communicate and interact more productively simply by using and reinforcing the skills, techniques, and processes discussed in this book (and others you develop). Even if they continue to fight, you will have at least helped them "fight better."

You can leave it at that as participants leave the mediation or consider asking questions or making suggestions to reinforce the learning and how that learning can be applied after mediation ends. For example, you might ask each to reflect on at least one skill, tool, or strategy they might use to support better communication. Doing so can get them to reflect on the need to change their behaviors, if only a little bit for their own self-preservation to make future encounters less contentious. In addition, you might suggest a few skills and techniques to remember from the mediation. For example:

"Please recall how we went through the process of listening to one another, taking time to reflect on what we heard from the other, asking clarifying questions as needed, and then responding based on what we heard. I think this will help in your future interactions."

"We made some progress in evaluating various options for resolving the issues you identified as important to you. You found some common ground on a few issues. I hope you can look back on that as a means for addressing some of the remaining issues that concern you."

Don't be preachy or judgmental. Instead, build lessons into statements of appreciation and praise for what the participants did accomplish. Remind them that they are capable of continuing the conversation and finding common ground on their own.

Remain Available to Assist

As an everyday mediator, you have more options for assisting participants than an external mediator does. If the participants valued your support and ethical, neutral process, you can mediate again if needed. If not, you can help find someone else without requiring them to explain their reasons. You can also offer coaching to help improve their communication and interactions, though this could affect your neutrality for future mediation. If coaching isn't appropriate, you can refer them to other resources. Your goal is to ensure they have the support they need moving forward.

Bottom line: you aren't leaving them in a lurch. Let them know you remain accessible in whatever ways will help them work through and improve their interpersonal relationship.

And if all goes well, they may be willing to meet again to resolve their conflict. That is when you need to capture the agreement.

Capture Agreements

When participants reach an agreement, you want to be sure they fully understand their commitments and know what they need to do to ensure that the agreement sticks. The mediation process can be draining, but resist the urge to wrap up without clarifying these commitments.

1. **Be specific about each participant's actions.**

What will they do, when, and how? Avoid vague agreements as they don't provide clear guidance on what needs to be done. For example:

| For an agreement between Laura and Barbara about use of cubicle space and Laura's daily visit with friends... | Instead of:

Laura will ask her friends to leave when it's time to get back to work. | State:

Laura will inform her friends she has to return to work after 10 minutes of conversation at the beginning of the day. |

For an agreement between Marcus and Sylvester about maintaining a common fence...	Instead of: Marcus will clean up after his dogs and Sylvester will keep his side of the fence clear of brush.	State: Marcus will clean up his side of the fence each time his dogs go potty—he will either scoop it up or blend it into the soil. Sylvester gives Marcus permission to do the same on his side of the fence. Sylvester will clear his side of the fence of debris and brush once a month.
For an agreement between a roof contractor and a homeowner about finishing the work and finalizing payment...	Instead of: Contractor will fix the slant of the gutter. Homeowner will pay a reduced amount on the remaining half of the payment due.	State: Contractor will return by November 15 to repair the gutter to ensure that it is angled properly to allow drainage. Upon completion of all work, homeowner will pay x, which reflects a 20% reduction of the original amount due of y as a result of delay and in compensation for accepting lower-grade shingles with a lesser warranty.

Agreements need clear timeframes, actions, and quality standards. It's important to articulate what participants will do to address other concerns as well, including communication, respect, trust, and consideration. In certain cases, framing actions and behaviors in tangible terms can help ensure that these intangible issues are addressed. For example:

- Barbara and Laura will meet for morning coffee once every two weeks to check in and address continuing concerns. They agree to meet together with their supervisor to discuss any issues they cannot resolve on their own.
- Marcus and Sylvester will hold a backyard picnic this summer along with their families and invite other neighbors to support neighborhood connection.

In the first example, misunderstandings between Laura and Barbara have led to mistrust due to a lack of face-to-face communication. Marcus and Sylvester may use a backyard picnic to heal their relationship after years of petty bickering. Though the picnic and regular meetings are tangible actions, they address deeper, intangible needs such as healing and community connection.

2. Ensure that the agreement includes participant commitments to absent third parties.
Many situations involve individuals or groups outside the four walls of the mediation who will be impacted by the agreement. This includes third parties both to whom the participants have an obligation and who themselves have obligations to the participants. Depending on the circumstances, they will need to know any or all of the following:

    I. That the matter has been resolved
    II. Specific action steps the participants are taking that the third party should be aware of
    III. The extent to which the third party may be asked or expected to do something in support of the agreement

Relevant third parties should know that the participants have found a way to move forward, without needing all the details. The goal is to protect confidentiality and allow participants to speak freely. If a third party insists on full details, it can undermine trust in the process. The participants should decide how to communicate this, either directly or through you. For many situations, the participants may feel that communicating items II and III is not necessary or that they can do so on their own. Therefore, succinctly communicating item I may be all that is necessary.

3. Include your commitments to the participants.
There are at least three people in a mediation: two participants (or more) and you. That means there are three people making commitments, not just two. The agreement must capture what you will do to finalize matters.

    As mentioned, you may assist with communicating to third parties, either via email or in person. Ensure that your involvement empowers participants rather than does the work for them. Your role is to facilitate and offer follow-up support, not to take over communication or strategy work. Participants may request a check-in meeting to address any issues, revise the agreement, or untangle lingering conflicts. It also helps with accountability as new agreements often require changes in behavior and habits.

    The timing of follow-up meetings depends on the purpose. For accountability, three to four weeks may be appropriate; for tracking implementation, one to two weeks is typically better. These meetings should be shorter than the initial mediation, or about an hour. It's often best to schedule them before concluding the mediation.

4. Record the agreement, as appropriate for the situation. As a mediator, you commit to documenting the agreement. Formal mediations often use templates outlining the context, terms, and participant signatures. In legal contexts, these agreements can be enforceable and serve as a basis for legal action if terms are unmet. Agreements to resolve interpersonal conflicts are not usually tied to litigation, but consequences can still arise, such as formal discipline from a supervisor. It's essential to capture the terms accurately and ensure that participants understand the seriousness and potential consequences of breaching the agreement. Mediators can record agreements in various ways, such as by typing them up on-site, reviewing with participants, and having them sign the final version before adjourning.

Using email to memorialize an agreement may be acceptable for many informal work-related mediations where concerns about legal action are minimal. If you're mediating in an organization, check with administrators or legal counsel for their preferred method. For informal mediations, participants often choose not to formalize agreements, feeling that a verbal understanding is sufficient; however, I offer this option whenever possible.

5. Celebrate.
Congratulations, you've successfully helped resolve the conflict! As you wrap up, outline any follow-up steps and thank the participants for trusting you. Acknowledge their effort, and if they thank you, humbly return the credit,

emphasizing that the success was theirs. Wish them well as they "exit the bus."

Celebrate the resolution but remember that the process was challenging. Though issues have been resolved, participants still may not feel overly close. A handshake, mutual appreciation, or casual chat is typical. However they leave the mediation—together or separately—doesn't reflect success or failure. Your celebration may be subtle, but always end on a positive, affirming note.

Conclude with Grace, Dignity, and Respect
Ending mediation positively is easy whenever a conflict has been resolved—but what if it hasn't? Some mediations end unresolved or in a vague middle ground. Participants must still "exit the bus" with dignity—but how?

Once progress has stalled, when is it time to end? Sometimes, participants will signal it clearly themselves, but often, it's up to you to wrap up. Before closing, assess whether a final push is worthwhile. If not, ensure that you're the last to reach that conclusion. If so, try—then end only when further effort is futile.

Like the person on that bumpy bus ride who's designated with helping others exit safely, consider what participants need when leaving unresolved. What do they fear? How do they want to be perceived?

Your role is to ease tensions, reinforce good behavior, and keep them mindful of each other's needs while fostering hope for future resolution. Always conclude with grace, dignity, and respect, even in difficult situations.

Start with Grace: Giving the Gift of Time, Space, and Understanding
When mediation stalls, it may be because participants fail to let down their guard. Despite efforts to encourage listening

Seventh Practice: Support a Dignified Exit

and compromise, they remain defensive, unaccustomed to a process that requires deference and mutual consideration. Now is the time to pause. They must reflect: Is continuing the fight worth the cost? Are concessions possible for peace? Every argument has been made, every option explored. At the very least, they now fully understand each other's concerns.

Encourage them to create space for reflection, even if resolution isn't immediate. Like a battlefield truce, stepping back allows them to assess whether the fight is worth its toll. Sometimes, distance leads to a lasting ceasefire.

Before concluding, if the situation permits, ask each participant to take a moment to suspend the high level of anxiety and emotion they are feeling and to reflect on the other's perspective on the situation and what the other needs in order to be able to resolve the dispute. They may do this quietly or perhaps they will be willing to articulate these understandings, even if they don't agree. Practically, they must find ways to interact with more respect, step back from demands, and seek greater understanding. The battle is paused—now they must decide what comes next.

Move to Dignity: Acknowledging Our Contribution and Seeing the Human in the Other

Though, as everyday mediators, we should model humility and vulnerability, participants often don't. If little progress has been made, it's likely because one or both refuse to see their role in the conflict. Without vulnerability—without being human—no real movement occurs.

Mediation humanizes conflict. When one participant shows humility or regret, or even apologizes, the other often reciprocates. They begin to see each other as human—capable of mistakes but also of change. This process restores dignity.

In unresolved conflicts, dignity is often lost, with participants attacking each other—and themselves—in the process. As mediation concludes, observe and, if appropriate, share how their actions have hindered resolution and diminished their own standing.

Encourage participants not only to express what they need but also to examine how their behaviors fuel resistance. Don't assume that they'll do this naturally—guide them. Keep the focus on the contributions that each is willing to acknowledge and the issues that keep the conflict alive—and don't allow them to point a finger back at the other person. Summarize key points and suggest that they remain mindful of these considerations as you conclude. Continued reflection beyond mediation is key to any hope of resolution.

End with Respect: Treating One Another with Positive Regard, in Good Times and Bad

Our actions and behaviors can contribute to conflict and resistance—and despite our best intentions, often end up showing a lack of respect. Though acknowledging this fact is important, real progress comes from making positive changes that demonstrate respect and foster reconciliation.

Again, if the situation permits, ask each participant to state one or two changes they might take to show positive regard for the other or to honor a request or need the other has articulated. These may not necessarily be monumental, but accept whatever ideas and suggestions they provide without judgment. Then, thank them for sharing and briefly summarize what each has stated. In healthy conflicts, participants naturally reach these realizations. Beyond resolving specific issues—such as contract terms or work processes—they often agree on actions to improve their

Seventh Practice: Support a Dignified Exit

relationship, reflecting mutual needs for respect, dignity, and even friendship.

In deeper conflicts, entrenched participants struggle to move past hurt and resentment. However, if they can recognize their role in the conflict, they may also identify small changes to rebuild trust and take tentative steps toward resolution.

Will it always be possible to end this way? Probably not. Your words and methods may be different, but the ideas expressed are worth noting. To the extent that disputing participants can be challenged to proceed with grace, dignity, and respect, no matter how difficult their relationship, the greater their chances are of moving toward resolution—eventually.

In mediation where participants remain unsettled, all you may be able to accomplish is to have them articulate a few changes they are willing to make. These may be very small changes. Beyond that, it may not be possible even to get them to make a verbal commitment to make the changes they have articulated. Perhaps all you can do is request that they do so. Yet perhaps the mere acknowledgement of their contribution to the conflict and hearing themselves articulate a few basic steps to change will result in a little more consideration, patience, and respect that they afford each other as they navigate their relationship without you.

You may never know. After mediation concludes, you must leave the rest to them—and with that, any chance of resolution to time, space, reflection, and grace.

Chapter 8 Reflective Exercise

My Mediation Journey (Reflections on a Mediation Experience)

This exercise offers a recap of the seven practices of everyday mediation, with questions to guide your reflection. It's both a tool and an inspiration for your journey in helping others address conflict. Whether you're new to mediation or experienced, use this guide to reflect on your own journey, analyze your experiences, and consider what you can apply to future situations. Use the template as is or pull specific items and question prompts for journaling as suits your preferences and needs. An example based on Sumiko's journey is provided in the resources section.

Participants:

Mediation Situation:

Other Relevant Issues:

Recognize the Call: Develop a Vision for Your Role as Everyday Mediator

Question prompts:

- What is my relationship to the participants?
- What was my role in this situation?
- How would I describe the call to which I responded?
- Did it come as a surprise or did I expect to be relied upon in this way?

My notes:

Respond in the Moment: Provide Immediacy and Attention to People in Conflict

Question prompts:

- What was the nature of the conflict that required a response?
- How did I respond initially to provide support?
- Was my response timely and appropriate?
- What, if anything, could I do differently to be more responsive in future situations?

My notes:

Offer a Seat: Provide a Safe Place to Meet

Question prompts:

- What did I do to prepare participants for mediation?
- How did I make it safe for them to discuss their concerns—with me and with each other?
- What skills, approaches, and strategies were helpful?
- What skills, approaches, and strategies should I develop further?

My notes:

Sit with Others: Create Environments for Talking, Listening, and Empathy Amid the Chaos

Question prompts:

- How did I support effective sharing and storytelling?
- What did I do to encourage listening and reflection?
- How did my framing of issues help them understand and begin to address what truly mattered to them?
- What could I have done differently?

My notes:

Share the Ride: Ceaselessly Support Others Through the Long Journey to Reconciliation

Question prompts:

- How did I manage unproductive reactions and behaviors?
- How did I help each participant adopt more collaborative behaviors?
- Was I appropriately deliberate and exhaustive in efforts to encourage collaboration? Too much/little?
- What skills do I need to further develop?

My notes:

Bring Transformative Power: Find, Support, and Exploit Breakthrough Moments

Question prompts:

- What were the breakthrough moments?
- What happened to support breakthrough?
- What did I do to support breakthrough?
- If no breakthrough, why, and was there anything I could have done differently?
- What skills and tools do I need to further develop?

My notes:

Support a Dignified Exit: Conclude with Grace, Dignity, and Respect, No Matter the Outcome

Question prompts:

- What was the outcome?
- If positive, in what way?
- If somewhat positive but with lingering issues, what remained unresolved?
- If wholly unresolved, why?
- Regardless of outcome, how did I foster grace, dignity, and respect?

My notes:

Final Thoughts/Comments

Question prompts:

- Ultimately, how do I feel about my efforts?
- In a few words, how would I describe my experience?
- How does this experience fit within or fulfill my broader vision as an everyday mediator?
- What can I build from to be more effective in future situations?

My notes:

Chapter 9

Conclusion: If We're Being Honest with Ourselves

And That's a Big "If"

If we are truly honest with ourselves, we know that conflict is unavoidable. It is woven right into the very fabric of all human relationships. It appears in our workplaces, our communities, our families, and even within ourselves. But if we are just as honest, we also know that how we engage with conflict determines whether it deepens the underlying division or leads to an amicable understanding.

Too often, we assume that conflict resolution is someone else's job—the job of experts, professionals, or those with specialized training. We tell ourselves that we aren't qualified, that we don't have the skills, that it's not our place. We have "more important things to do" in our rushed lives. So we wait for someone more experienced, more knowledgeable, more neutral to step in. *Surely, someone else will do it and be more qualified to do so.*

But if we're still being honest, we also know that we don't need a title or a certificate to help people find common ground. We don't need years of experience to be a steady presence in moments of tension. What we need is the courage to show up, the willingness to listen, and the humility to create space for others.

Everyday mediation, at its core, is not about techniques or frameworks—it's about being present for others. It's about offering a seat at the table (or on a bus)—both literally and figuratively—when people are lost in conflict, sitting with them, and sharing the ride.

Michelle understood that. She didn't wait for permission. She didn't consult a manual. She didn't worry about whether she was "qualified." She simply stepped in and did what she could, in the way she knew how, with what she had. And because she did, she changed everything for me in that moment.

That's the lesson. Everyday mediation isn't about being an expert. It's about being human.

Why More of Us Need to Be Every Third Person

We live in a world that loves to take sides. Pick an issue—politics, business, relationships, social justice—and you'll find deeply entrenched camps, each convinced of their own rightness, unwilling to listen, unwilling to budge. The problem isn't just that we disagree; it's that we refuse to engage. We refuse to consider that another perspective might have value. We refuse to acknowledge that compromise isn't weakness—it's wisdom.

Rarely do the best solutions come from one side "winning" and the other losing. Lasting solutions—whether in workplaces, communities, or families—come when people set aside their rigidity long enough to recognize shared goals. But that can't happen in an environment of stridency, blame, and unchecked ego.

And that's where the third person comes in. Imagine the world is divided into three groups:

1. Those on one side of a conflict
2. Those on the other side
3. Those who step in to help bridge the divide

Right now, the third group is far too small. There aren't enough people willing to step forward and say, "Let's try something different."

If more of us took on that role, if more of us chose to engage instead of standing back, the world would be a different place. Conflicts would still exist, but they would be met with more curiosity than hostility, more listening than lecturing, more problem-solving than posturing.

The world doesn't need more side-takers. It needs more bridge-builders.

The Choice in Front of Us

The need for mediators isn't theoretical. People in conflict aren't some abstract idea—they're real. They're in your office, struggling with a difficult colleague. They're in your community, feeling unheard. They're in your family, carrying wounds that never healed. They're right in front of you, right now, looking for a way forward.

And you have a choice.

You can ignore them. You can assume that it's not your problem. You can let them figure it out on their own. Or you can offer a seat. You can ask a question. You can hold space for a conversation that wouldn't otherwise happen. And in doing so, you can change the outcome.

Not every conflict will be resolved. Not every situation will end in reconciliation. But every time someone chooses to step into the third role, the possibility of resolution grows. Every time someone creates space for understanding, the chance for peace expands.

The question isn't whether you have the skill. It's whether you have the willingness to try.

What It Means to Be Honest with Ourselves

I wrote this book because I believe wholeheartedly in everyday mediation. I believe that helping people navigate conflict isn't just the work of professionals—it's the work of all of us. I believe that we are all capable of holding space for hard conversations, if we choose to.

And yet I also know that choosing to do so isn't easy.

Being honest with ourselves means acknowledging that stepping into the role of mediator is uncomfortable. It's vulnerable. It means being willing to be wrong, to be challenged, to not have all the answers. It means resisting the instinct to "fix" things and instead sitting with discomfort, guiding others to their own solutions. It also means recognizing that we won't always get it right.

I spent years trying to be the perfect mediator. I trained; I studied models; I worked tirelessly to refine my approach. And yet the most important lesson I learned wasn't about technique—it was about presence. It was about showing up as a person first, before ever worrying about being an "expert."

That's what Michelle did for me. That's what we can do for others.

You Are the Expert You Need to Be

Mediation isn't a job. It's a way of being in the world. It's a choice we make, over and over again, to engage rather than retreat, to hold space rather than take sides, to seek solutions rather than reinforce divisions.

If enough of us make that choice, it will change more than individual conflicts. It will change entire cultures—or, in my optimistic view, the world. I don't pretend to have an answer to the world's problems, much less the problems in our country or in our communities, workplaces, schools, neighborhoods, or families. But I have suggested that if enough of us start thinking and acting in terms of being an everyday mediator, we can bring positive change to the world. Perhaps I'm being too bold here—but I honestly don't think so.

If we're being honest with ourselves, the question isn't whether we *can* do this. It's whether we *will*.

If you take nothing else from this book, take this: You don't need permission to mediate. You don't need to wait until you feel "qualified." You don't need to be flawless, fearless, or perfectly impartial.

You just need to care.
You just need to be willing to listen.
You just need to offer a seat.

Resources

Chapter 1

"Journal Prompts for Developing as an Authentic, Everyday Mediator" Exercise Example

Traits, characteristics, and qualities that I currently possess:

- **Empathetic and supportive:** Calm, nonreactive, and a good listener when others are stressed or troubled
- **Passionate and focused:** Demonstrates deep commitment and singular focus when pursuing something meaningful
- **Empowering and hardworking:** Loyal, self-reliant, and dedicated to helping others grow through teaching and skill sharing
- **Driven by excellence:** Holds high standards, rejects mediocrity, and consistently strives for quality in all areas of life

Traits, characteristics, and qualities of people who most annoy me:

- **Manipulative behavior:** Dislike for pushy, schmoozy individuals who manipulate others for selfish gain
- **Lack of integrity:** Annoyed by insecure, self-indulgent people who lack tact and professional decorum
- **Abuse of power:** Frustrated by bullies who ignore boundaries and seek to influence outcomes unfairly
- **Enablers in leadership:** Low tolerance for leaders who are blind to bad behavior or reward arrogance over integrity

Traits, characteristics, and qualities to which I aspire:

- **Greater patience and presence:** Desires to be more patient and less anxious about daily distractions
- **Stronger focus and assertiveness:** Aims to improve discipline and be more direct in resolving conflicts
- **Internal confidence and humility:** Inspired by people who are grounded and self-assured and lead with humility
- **Collaborative spirit:** Strives to both give and receive support generously, helping others grow while growing personally

What this exercise means for me and what conclusions I draw:

When people who push my buttons refuse to listen or take "no" for an answer, or are pushy and manipulative, perhaps they are being as passionate as I am but express it quite differently. They loathe mediocrity just as I do. Perhaps the myopic leaders who annoy me have similar interests as I do in enabling and empowering others but focus their energies on individuals who are brash and arrogant without awareness of their negative impacts.

Those I admire most are generous, confident, assertive, and not afraid to ask for help, whereas those who annoy me are unapologetic about getting their needs met in an assertive yet selfish manner. Yet perhaps I'm just as selfish when focused on my passions. I say I'm self-reliant, but is this self-indulgence if taken to an extreme? Still, I don't see a place for "schmooziness," cowardliness, or heedless reliance on "higher-ups" to get one's way without taking responsibility for one's actions or regard for others.

Reflection on biases and distortions I must consider when mediating:

I must not reject out of hand myopic leaders and abrasive individuals who, with the help of mediation, might be able to broaden their perspective about how their actions are hurting others. At the same time, if their actions and behaviors are so "over the top" without apparent ability to self-reflect, I should probably not suggest mediation with individuals in weaker positions, particularly where significant power differentials are involved. Even where mediation might otherwise be appropriate, such as between coequal business partners, I may need to consider whether I can fairly support a brash, take-no-prisoners participant if I can't get past my biases about their behaviors.

Chapter 2

"Discover Your Mediation Wherevers" Exercise Example

Role (Describe)	Relationships and Situations (Current or Possible) Where Mediation Skills Will Be Useful
Manager or team leader: *manager for accounts receivable; leader for front desk; CEO; COO; school principal; coach, etc.*	*Bill and Katie are arguing about project responsibilities; 5th-grade teachers may have a problem with the new grading requirements.*
Team member or peer: *coworker at XYX, Inc.; pitcher for softball team, etc.*	*Coworkers are uncomfortable with Ned, new team member; Kaitlin and Margie don't sit together anymore at lunch.*
Institutional representative: *employee-relations representative; manager of equal-opportunity office; corporate ombuds, etc.*	*Max is calling again about disciplining Judy; employees always want to file grievances; employees don't know how to talk with abrasive coworkers.*

Service professional: *return desk at ABC, Inc. retail outlet; attending nurse in emergency; bailiff; court-appointed guardian ad litem*	*Customers may become angry at any moment; Mrs. Knox's family doesn't understand Dr. Kaufman's treatment plan; customers don't appreciate the manager's explanations.*
Friend, family member, or neighbor: *sister, uncle, dad, stepmother; foster parent; lives next door to Trish and behind Marwan; friends with Trish, Brandi, and Harrianna*	*Oh, boy, it's Christmas time again; Marwan and Trish can't agree on who should trim the fence line; can my girlfriends for once go to the movies and not fight?*
Good person on bus (or elsewhere): *ride bus #9; take 7:45 train every morning; shop at EZ Mart grocery store; bowl at Spares & Strikes*	*They need to stop arguing and sit down; Josephine (cash register) seems to be having a difficult time with that customer.*
Other: *volunteer Tuesday nights at food pantry*	*It's unpleasant volunteering because Kate and Meaghan are always squabbling.*

Note: this example illustrates roles for multiple individuals, not a single individual.

Chapter 3

"Prepare to 'Respond in the Moment'" Exercise Example

Participants:

- Kim, my supervisor
- Ashley, coworker, former direct report, reports to Kim now

General notes on the conflict situation: *Tension between Ashley and Kim. It's been simmering for months and blew up today. I probably should have done something sooner to respond, but I didn't know about Kim's situation at the time.*

- How immediate is the need to respond? Determine the urgency, then jot down the kind of statements and messages you might share to respond at the appropriate moment. Refer back to the first section on the "Spectrum of Needs" for further insight. If you have already dealt with the situation, reflect on what you did and what you might do differently in the future.

    - Evolving need ("I wonder..." or similar messages and statements)
    - Evolved need ("I notice..." or similar messages and statements)
    - Urgent need ("Please take a seat" or similar messages and statements)

    Ashley: *This is an urgent need, though I saw it coming and might have done something earlier. I had to tell Ashley that her behavior was inappropriate in the meeting with Kim. I told her that she needed to calm down. She was angry, and I told her that quitting was not the answer, but she needed to talk things through with Kim.*

Kim: *Also an urgent need. I didn't expect tears or to learn about her stress regarding her daughter. I didn't know how to respond to her crying, so I said nothing. I explained that she needed to talk things through with Ashley. Thankfully, she agreed.*

I think it is wise to wait until tomorrow to talk about the situation. They were not prepared to talk today. Plus, it was at the end of the day.

- How will you suggest mediation or a mediation-type communication process? Look back at "Suggest a Different Approach" and consider the "talking points" you'll use to encourage the individuals to sit down and engage in the appropriate conversation.

    Ashley: *I told her I would help her express her concerns in a way that perhaps she hasn't been able to yet. She is so angry, so I need to help her state her concerns more calmly.*

    Kim: *I explained that we need to put aside our work for a moment to talk things through. She was reluctant, but I think I convinced her it was at least worth a try. She seemed drained and exhausted, so perhaps she was willing to agree to anything at that point.*

- What resistance do you anticipate? Look back at "Expect and Address Resistance" and jot down the specific kinds of resistance that each individual might offer, such as concerns about the effectiveness of the process, lack of trust in the other person, your ability to assist, etc. and how you might respond.

    Ashley: *I got her to agree at least to meet tomorrow, but I'm not sure she'll be able to listen to Kim when we do meet. I need to explain that going off in a huff and threatening to quit won't do anyone any good. I need to help her understand that Kim is a different person than Ben, so she'll need to find a way to understand Kim better. There is also no justification for placing blame. I don't think she'll be inappropriate like she was today, but still, I need to be prepared for any reactions and show her that remaining calm and listening are going to be important, particularly if she wants Kim to listen to her.*

    Kim: *I need to help her understand that sharing more about herself might help us understand the pressures she's under. She needs to feel comfortable that sharing her concerns is okay, even if she is our boss. She needs to also feel that she's not being judged by an impossible standard—she's not Ben, and that's okay. I'm also concerned that she may be too focused on work issues, so I need to help her understand that talking through your concerns is the best way to get back to dealing with work issues.*

- What preliminary plan might you suggest for getting them to the table? Where? When? For how long? Look back at "Get People to the Table (or the Coffee Shop)" and jot down issues, concerns, and logistical considerations for arranging the appropriate time, place, and space.

    Where? *I think the coffee shop is a good place to meet. There may be a little noise, but we can tune it out. It's casual and relaxed, and that's what I want to promote.*

    When? *Morning, after Kim has time to get her daughter to school. I sent out-of-office messages and managed the schedule for tomorrow, so we don't need to feel rushed.*

    For how long? *At least an hour, perhaps a little longer. We'll see how things go and if we are able to stay longer if we need to. Otherwise, I'll suggest that we reconvene soon somewhere else.*

    Other logistical considerations: *If it's too noisy or turns out to be distracting, we'll have to find another place quickly. If need be, we'll come back to the office, though I'd prefer not to meet in such a sterile environment. I want them to feel more relaxed.*

Chapter 4

Introductory Statement Sample Script

Thank you for meeting today. I appreciate your willingness and courage to meet together to discuss this matter. I know it has been a challenge, and your willingness to meet says a lot about your commitment to resolving this matter. Thanks also for placing your trust in me to facilitate your conversation. Your trust is crucial, and I will want to know if at any time I am not living up to that expectation. Let me lay out a few matters regarding the process we are utilizing today, as well as expectations and guidelines I'd like to suggest to ensure a productive meeting.

First, I'm here to help you communicate so that you both feel listened to and understood. I am not here to make, suggest, or insist on any decision. What you decide today, or whether you reach any decision, is up to you. I am not a judge or decision-maker and have no authority to force a decision.

Second, this is a confidential process. That means what we discuss today stays in the room. To the extent others may need to know the outcomes of our discussion, or you want others to be aware, we will not share such details except by mutual consent.

Third, I am not taking sides. My intent is to be neutral and impartial. That means I will not do or say anything that suggests a bias toward or that advocates for one person over the other. I will make every attempt to ensure that you each feel fully heard and have every opportunity to respond to the other person. If you feel that I am not acting in a neutral, impartial manner, please let me know immediately.

In the interest of ensuring neutrality and impartiality, I have discussed with each of you my prior knowledge of the situation. This includes [share details, as relevant]. In addition, we have discussed prior relationships and connections we've had that could potentially be perceived as influencing my perspective. These include [share details, as relevant]. You each agreed that these issues would not affect your confidence in my ability to facilitate this conversation in a fair and impartial manner. Is that still how you feel? [After participants give assent:] Great!

Let's take a moment to suggest a few norms for talking today. I want to encourage you to fully listen to each other's comments, ideas, and perspectives before responding. That means not interrupting while the other person is talking. I also encourage you to consider fully what the other person has said before responding. I may at times even ask you to reframe in your own words what you heard the other person say. This will help you understand the extent to which the other person has understood you before being expected to listen and respond.

Beyond that, I don't have any other suggestions, but we can offer additional suggestions as we proceed. If you have any suggestions to offer now, please do so.

[After discussion, if any:]: Okay, it seems we've arrived at a basic understanding of how we'll communicate. I just want to confirm: do you each agree with these norms for talking and to abide by them? [Upon obtaining agreement]: Great. Thank you.

Please also let me know at any time when you'd like to take a break. A break can help when things become uncomfortable, you feel triggered in some way, or need time to think about matters. Also, I may call a break so that I can speak separately with one of you if I sense you are having difficulty raising an issue or if there is a matter that you shared with me confidentially that might be beneficial to bring up but that isn't my place to raise. My purpose in meeting separately is to support the process and help you communicate effectively. The last thing I want you to think is that I am colluding with the other person or taking a side. If this becomes a concern, let me know. You can also request, of course, to meet with me separately.

In a moment, I will ask you to begin sharing. Before we do, are there any questions, concerns, or other matters either of you would like to discuss?

[After discussion, if any:] Thank you again for meeting today. Let's begin by understanding each other's perspective on the matter. Who would like to start?

Chapter 5

"Capture Stories for Future Exploration" Exercise Example

Participant: Randi	Participant: Robert
Notes, issues, concerns, key points, etc.	Notes, issues, concerns, key points, etc.
Meetings waste of time—stopped attending—email easier	Randi not open to team input—defensive
Hates small talk (Robert loves it)	"Team"—interpersonal connections important
"Team"—business purpose; not needed for work (event planning); independent Robert doesn't like ideas—so she stopped sharing Etc.	Email not always best—need meetings to discuss plans and ideas Randi doesn't fit in culture Etc.

Randi's Interests	Robert's Interests
Efficient communication (i.e., via email instead of in-person)	Effective communication (i.e., in-person provides more clarity)
Privacy regarding personal life	Connecting with others to support team cohesion
Appreciation of new ideas	Collaboration to produce the best ideas
Business purpose for team interactions	Fostering team cohesiveness is a business purpose

Chapter 6

"Assess/Reflect/Plan Road Map" Exercise Example

Assess

What am I observing about each participant's behaviors and conflict styles? How do they respond when challenged? What are the consistent patterns that keep each stuck in conflict? (Note: consider fight, flight, and compromise behaviors or describe participant behaviors in other ways that you find helpful.)

Participant: Rex	Participant: Judith
Competitive—push, push, push	Professionally competitive, prefers collaborating
Reactive when challenged, always on defense	Consummate professional, reticent to reveal personal feelings, keeps focus on interest of firm (not good)
Not a good listener	
Compromising—pushes until he has something to lose (when "caught")	Prone to compromise as standard business approach (while torn up inside)
Etc.	Etc.

Reflect

What are the situations and scenarios where the participants clashed before? What was happening? How did each respond? What situations might arise in mediation? How might these situations threaten possibilities for collaboration? How might they present opportunities?

- *Rex thinks that Judith's behavioral expectations diminish him as a lawyer (being a bastard makes him a great lawyer).*
- *Judith is at the limits of toleration, having tolerated Rex's behaviors far too long.*
- *Judith needs to loosen up to express emotional and relationship costs; Rex needs to be persuaded to listen deeply and to demonstrate understanding of intangible loss and costs.*
- *Compromise solution is possible but ultimately damaging to Rex, Judith, Thomas, and the firm.*
- *Etc.*

Plan

What skills, approaches, and strategies might I need to respond to the behaviors and situations I've described? (Think in terms of specific scenarios and the specific skill, approach, or strategy you may need to use. Keep the plan flexible in order to prepare for matters you won't be able to anticipate.)

- *During mediation, spend time with (1) Rex to ensure that he stays settled and able to walk through what he's hearing Judith say before going off on defense mode; need to bring him back when this happens; and (2) Judith when she is too much the consummate professional; inquire to get her to explain more "why" concerns are so important to her, not just the firm.*

- *Guide them to see how their continued path of compromise is not only unsatisfactory but also potentially devastating; don't tell, but have them see for themselves through inquiry, reflection, etc.*

Chapter 7

"Prepare for Breakthrough Opportunities" Exercise Example

Preparing for Breakthrough (Sample—Stacy's Notes)	
Participant A: *Annalise*	
Participant B: *Lexi*	
Conflict Situation: *Lexi wants Annalise to collaborate on a training project, but Annalise refuses due to past experiences where she felt bullied and her reputation suffered. Though Lexi knows Annalise has concerns, she doesn't grasp the full impact of her actions. The project is crucial to the company and their bosses.*	
Positions: What are the hard-and-fast, "yes or no" positions each participant is holding onto? **Why** is each position so important to the participant? **Why** are alternatives to this position **not** possible?	
Annalise: *Doesn't want to work again with Lexi under any circumstance.* *Believes she won't be treated as a "partner."*	Lexi: *Having Annalise on the project is "imperative."* *There shouldn't be a problem working with her again; it's just business.*

Lexi wants to "control" her and the full project; Annalise doesn't want her as de facto boss again.	Has "business reasons" for managing the process, though not how Annalise would want.

Interests: What interests (issues, needs, concerns, values, etc.) do you perceive are important to each participant that lay beneath the positions they are taking?

Think in terms of interests that, if met, would help participants move from hard-and-fast, "yes or no" positions to possibilities for finding common ground with each other.

Annalise:	Lexi:
Respect as full partner	Particular about how projects are done
Never to be bullied and manipulated again	Difficulty trusting others to relinquish control
Difficulty trusting Lexi	
Needs to feel control (to complain, quit, etc.) if Lexi behaves the same as she did before	Needs someone to help complete project
	Insecurity, fear about anything reflecting badly on her

Framing Statement: Considering their varying interests, how would you frame the issues in a compelling way that provides a basis for helping the participants attempt to resolve the matter?

Issue 1: How can Annalise feel respected and included while ensuring that Lexi trusts that the project aligns with sales-department goals?

Issue 2: How do they define the working parameters of the project to ensure that Issue 1 is fulfilled?

Issue 3: What can they do to restore trust and ensure against repeating past experiences so they can effectively work together to meet the business needs defined by the project?

Issue 4: What options do they have if they don't work together on the project or if difficulties arise in their working relationships in the course of executing the project?

(add additional issues as needed)

Options and Alternatives for Resolution: What options have the participants suggested, or might they consider, to resolve each issue you've identified (as captured in your framing statement)?

- How will these options be evaluated? What criteria will be used?
- Which options are more viable than others?

Annalise:	Lexi:
- Refuses to work with Lexi and face the consequences (quit job if necessary) - Lexi acknowledges past behaviors and apologizes - Lexi agrees to refrain from repeating prior behaviors or faces consequences - Any inappropriate behavior gives Annalise license to seek support from Gordon - Lexi provides full transparency, including full participation with and access to clients - Negotiates parameters of project before beginning, with Gordon and Pratibha involved	- Acknowledges past difficult relationship but does not agree that behavior was inappropriate - Proceeds without Annalise but ensures that Pratibha understands impacts and that she isn't blamed - Proceeds with project as defined by sales directors without prior consultation with Annalise; Annalise agrees to her role as is - Annalise accepts "business reasons" for not having further access to clients; her role is different but still important; defines "partnership" accordingly

• Takes incremental steps conditioned on Lexi's behavior (e.g., show trust in first steps and don't "run to Momma," and Annalise takes next step to support project, and so on) • Reviews progress incrementally with consultation with Gordon and Pratibha	• Negotiates parameters of project before beginning; we are two mature adults, don't need bosses involved • Any complaints about the other will first be addressed with that person before going to bosses

Impasse: What resistance is each participant expressing (verbally or implicitly) that may prevent them from accepting an option or proposal?

What tools, strategies, and approaches might you utilize to help the participant overcome this resistance? (Note: if resistance is deeper than a legitimate struggle with impasse, such as lack of good faith, consider strategies in the next chapter, "Support a Dignified Exit.")

Annalise:	Lexi:
• Can't risk being bullied and manipulated again; if not supported by management this time, then won't play	• Pride about acknowledging past behaviors was abrasive or she's acted in any other way than professionally

• *Hard to believe trust can be restored with Lexi; doesn't believe Lexi is capable*	• *Fundamentally not trusting of anyone to relinquish control of project* • *Pervasive insecurity of involving higher-ups and exposing her weaknesses*

Agreements: What tentative agreements are possible to resolve the issues you've identified (as captured in the framing statement)? (Note: keep track of these for developing the final agreement.)

1. *Lexi acknowledges past challenges but doesn't apologize. Both agree to address concerns directly before escalating to their bosses.*

2. *Project progress pauses until Annalise is up to speed. They will define Annalise's role, access, and communication plan, with final approval from Gordon and Pratibha.*

3. *Monthly check-ins with Gordon and Pratibha will track progress and address concerns, with additional meetings as needed.*

(add additional items as needed)

Notes: Use this space to make notes about other aspects of the conflict that may help you in mediating. In particular, consider possible moments and opportunities that might occur for which you can "push" or "pull" participants toward breakthrough.

I need to encourage Annalise to share her experiences so Lexi understands their impact while ensuring that she feels safe speaking up. Lexi shows little emotion or empathy, so I must find ways to prompt her to acknowledge Annalise's concerns. Both need clarity on the potential outcomes of Annalise working with Lexi—or refusing.

Chapter 8

Sample Written Mediation Agreement Template

Date: [record date of agreement, not when mediation occurred]

Mediator: [name, address, phone, email, etc.]
_____
_____
_____

Participant:	Participant:
[name, address, phone, email, etc.]	[name, address, phone, email, etc.]
_____	_____
_____	_____

[Participant A] and [Participant B] met with [Mediator] on [date mediation occurred] to discuss [brief statement, such as "their working relationship," "a conflict concerning their common fence line," "a dispute involving repairs to Ms. Wilson's roof," etc.]. They have agreed to the following:

- List all items agreed to. Be as specific as possible. (Note example regarding fence-line dispute.)
    - Marcus will clean up his side of the fence each time his dogs go potty—he will either scoop it up or blend it into the soil.
    - Sylvester gives Marcus permission to do the same on his side of the fence.

- Sylvester will clear his side of the fence of debris and brush once a month.
  -
  -

- This agreement, the mediation, and all matters and details discussed will remain confidential between them and the mediator and not shared with any other person, except by mutual consent.

- By mutual consent, only the following details will be shared with [relevant third parties]:
  -
  -

- [Mediator] will do the following: [include details pertaining to concluding the mediation process, such as notice to relevant third parties, scheduling a follow-up meeting, etc.]

This concludes the mediation. Thank you for the opportunity to assist you in this matter. Please let me know how I can assist you in the future.

Signed: [Participant A]   Signed: [Participant B]
Printed name: _____   Printed name: _____

Mediator: _____

Chapter 8

"My Mediation Journey (Reflections on a Mediation Experience)" Exercise Example

Participants: Maggie, Sam

Mediation Situation: Conflict between two board members over whether to formally launch nonprofit; Maggie ready to go; Sam is cautious

Other Relevant Issues: Other board members also play a role

Recognize the Call: Develop a Vision for Your Role as Everyday Mediator

> Question prompts: What is my relationship to the participants? What was my role in this situation? How would I describe the call to which I responded? Did it come as a surprise, or did I expect to be relied upon in this way?

I'm secretary for the board and work with Maggie on a daily basis. I've observed Sam and Maggie in conflict over a couple months. It finally escalated at a board meeting. I've wanted to be a mediator but didn't see my role in this situation until Chrystal "pushed" me. That was a surprise!

Respond in the Moment: Provide Immediacy and Attention to People in Conflict

> Question prompts: What was the nature of the conflict that required a response? How did I

respond initially to provide support? Was my response timely and appropriate? What, if anything, could I do differently to be more responsive in future situations?

Maggie is so passionate but has trouble listening. Sam gets frustrated and resorts to sarcasm. Both have good ideas, and we need them. Sam can't quit but may anyway. I'm the novice in this group, so I didn't feel I could say anything. When things blew up and then Chrystal challenged me, I was scared and didn't know what to do. I'm glad I spoke up when I did, but I need to be more assertive and confident in the future. I could have played a more active role earlier in the conflict.

Offer a Seat: Provide a Safe Place to Meet

Question prompts: What did I do to prepare participants for mediation? How did I make it safe for them to discuss their concerns—with me and each other? What skills, approaches, and strategies were helpful? What skills, approaches, and strategies should I develop further?

There really wasn't time to prepare. Things sort of evolved. We tried to be supportive and understanding while we also challenged them to confront the situation. I started with my observations and telling them that they needed to step back from their arguments. I'm glad we stayed late; otherwise, we might not have returned (or at least Sam might not have). Maggie and Sam seemed okay with talking through their concerns. They trusted us. If I had said something earlier, such as at the previous meeting, or tried to express my concerns with Maggie, we might have avoided the blow-up, but who knows. I need to be less anxious. I can learn from Chrystal on that.

Sit with Others: Create Environments for Talking, Listening, and Empathy Amid the Chaos

> Question prompts: How did I support effective sharing and storytelling? What did I do to encourage listening and reflection? How did my framing of issues help them understand and begin to address what truly mattered to them? What could I have done differently?

I told them I was frustrated. An outside mediator probably wouldn't do that, but this situation was different. They seemed okay with it and started listening. Maggie didn't disagree about her struggles with listening and settling down when others are trying to help her. Sam didn't dare argue about being sarcastic. They didn't want to accept what the other was saying, but we kept at it, and I think they started to see how they were frustrating each other. I guess that's the main thing: keep at it until they either start to understand or decide to quit.

Share the Ride: Ceaselessly Support Others Through the Long Journey to Reconciliation

> Question prompts: How did I manage unproductive reactions and behaviors? How did I help each participant adopt more collaborative behaviors? Was I appropriately deliberate and exhaustive in efforts to encourage collaboration? Too much/little? What skills do I need to further develop?

They are both high-strung, especially Maggie. Chrystal helped a lot. She kept reinforcing the need for each to settle down and let the other person speak. Again, I need to be more assertive when someone becomes reactive. I suppose I did okay asking the right questions and getting them to talk through their issues. I could always learn more about asking the right questions.

Bring Transformative Power: Find, Support, and Exploit Breakthrough Moments

> Question prompts: What were the breakthrough moments? What happened to support breakthrough? What did I do to support breakthrough? If there was no breakthrough, why, and was there anything I could have done differently? What skills and tools do I need to further develop?

I'm not sure a breakthrough occurred. We did everything we could to ensure that Sam and Maggie had a clear picture of what each was feeling and needed. They know what they need to do now. I hope Sam stays on the board, but it isn't as though he is making a decision without full knowledge of who Maggie is and how she behaves, right or wrong. I tried to push them to a decision, so that was my "rookie mistake." I can't just expect things to happen magically. Practicing more patience would help.

Support a Dignified Exit: Conclude with Grace, Dignity, and Respect, No Matter the Outcome

> Question prompts: What was the outcome? If positive, in what way? If somewhat positive but with lingering issues, what remained unresolved? If

wholly unresolved, why? Regardless of outcome, how did I foster grace, dignity, and respect?

The evening ended calmly. It sure didn't start that way. Maggie and Sam have a lot to think about, as we all do. I liked how Chrystal framed things at the end. I think it's a good idea that Sam and Maggie do something to get back to having a respectful relationship. I'd hate to have them continuing with all that resentment. Maggie still needs Sam and the support of his firm, no matter what Sam decides to do. We'll still need to work with them as well.

Final Thoughts/Comments:

Question prompts: Ultimately, how do I feel about my efforts? In a few words, how would I describe my experience? How does this experience fit within or fulfill my broader vision as an everyday mediator? What can I build from to be more effective in future situations?

Exhausted and exhilarated. I'm glad Chrystal pushed me. I may not sleep tonight. There's so much to think about. Is law school the right thing, or do I want to do something else? I need to talk with Chrystal to get more ideas. For now, I need to speak up more at board meetings.

Endnotes

1. The *Model Standards of Conduct for Mediators* were developed to provide guidance to mediators of legal disputes but are broadly applicable to mediation in multiple contexts. *Model Standards of Conduct for Mediators*, accessed April 5, 2025, https://cadreworks.org/resources/model-standards-conduct-mediators.
2. Jimmy Carter, as quoted in "10 Inspiring Jimmy Carter Quotes for Living a Better Life," Biography, accessed March 17, 2025, https://www.biography.com/political-figures/g43103873/jimmy-carter-quotes.
3. Consider these references related to conflict coaching: Laura Crawshaw, *Grow Your Spine & Manage Abrasive Leadership Behavior: A Guide for Those Who Manage Bosses Who Bully* (Executive Insight Press, 2023); Tricia S. Jones and Ross Brinkert, *Conflict Coaching: Conflict Management Strategies and Skills for the Individual* (Thousand Oaks, CA: Sage Publications, Inc., 2008); Cinnie Noble, *Conflict Management Coaching: The CinergyTM Model* (CINERGYTM Coaching, 2012).
4. The International Ombuds Association (IOA) is the leading association for resources, training, and professional development for ombuds. International Ombuds Association, accessed April 4, 2025, https://www.ombudsassociation.org/.
5. For a comprehensive discussion of details covered when beginning mediation, refer to Moore, Christopher M., *The Mediation Process: Practical Strategies for Resolving Conflict*, 4th ed. (San Francisco: Jossey-Bass, 2014), 301-324.
6. For additional information on empathic listening, refer to: Stephen R. Covey, *The 7 Habits of Highly Effective People*, special ed. (New York: Simon & Schuster, 2020); Kenneth Cloke and Joan Goldsmith, *Resolving Conflicts at Work: Ten Strategies for Everyone at Work*, 3rd ed. (San Francisco: Jossey-Bass, 2011); Matthew McKay, Martha Davis, and Patrick Fanning, *How to Communicate: The Ultimate Guide to Improving Your Personal and Professional Relationships*, 3rd ed. (MJF Books, 2017).
7. Merriam-Webster, s.v. "Empathy," accessed March 12, 2025, https://www.merriam-webster.com/dictionary/empathy.
8. Jeanne M. Brett, *Negotiating Globally: How to Negotiate Deals, Resolve Disputes, and Make Decisions Across Cultural Boundaries*, 3rd ed. (San Francisco: Jossey-Bass, 2014); Hazel Rose Markus and Alana Conner, *Clash!: How to Thrive in a Multicultural World* (New York: Plume,

2014); David C. Thomas and Kerr Inkson, *Cultural Intelligence: Surviving and Thriving in the Global Village*, 3rd ed. (Oakland, CA: Berrett-Koehler Publishers, Inc., 2017).

9. For further insights comparing discussion, dialogue, and debate, refer to: Mark Gerzon, *Leading through Conflict: How Successful Leaders Transform Differences into Opportunities* (Boston: Harvard Business School Press, 2006); William Isaacs, *Dialogue and the Art of Thinking Together: A Pioneering Approach to Communicating in Business and in Life* (New York: Currency, 1999); Daniel Yankelovich, *The Magic of Dialogue: Transforming Conflict into Cooperation* (New York: Simon & Schuster, 1999).

10. Isaacs, 42.

11. The five behaviors commonly used to describe conflict responses are avoiding, accommodating, competing, compromising, and collaborating, based on the Thomas-Kilmann Conflict Mode Instrument (TKI). Individuals can take the TKI to identify their preferred responses to conflict. Kilmann Diagnostics, accessed April 6, 2025, https://kilmanndiagnostics.com. See also: Ralph H. Kilmann, *Mastering the Thomas-Kilmann Conflict Mode Instrument* (Newport Coast, CA: Kilmann Diagnostics, 2023).

12. The dynamics of fear and "fight or flight" responses are discussed in various contexts in the following references: Brandon Black and Shayne Hughes, *Ego Free Leadership: Ending the Unconscious Habits that Hijack Your Business* (Austin, TX: Greenleaf Book Group Press, 2017); Mark Goulston, *Just Listen: Discover the Secret to Getting Through to Absolutely Anyone* (New York: American Management Association, 2010); Joseph Grenny et al., *Crucial Conversations: Tools for Talking When Stakes are High*, 3rd ed. (New York: McGraw-Hill, 2021).

13. Stephen R. Covey popularized the concept of adopting a collaborative mindset with "Habit 4: Think Win-Win" in *The 7 Habits of Highly Effective People*. He further discussed this and related concepts in: Stephen R. Covey, *The 8th Habit: From Effectiveness to Greatness* (New York: Free Press, 2004); Stephen R. Covey, *The 3rd Alternative: Solving Life's Most Difficult Problems* (New York: Free Press, 2011).

14. Adapted from Zena D. Zumeta, "Framing Issues in Mediation: An Advanced Workshop," Association for Conflict Resolution (ACR) Annual Conference, Orlando, FL (October 15–18, 2003), reported in Paula Young, "Overcoming Impasse in Mediation: A Short Literature Review," Mediate.com (July 12, 2004), accessed April 6, 2025, https://mediate.com/overcoming-impasse-in-mediation-a-short-literature-review.

15. Roger Fisher, William Ury, and Bruce Patton, *Getting to Yes: Negotiating Agreement Without Giving In*, 3rd ed. (New York: Penguin Books 2011); Roger Fisher and Danny Ertel, *Getting Ready to Negotiate: The*

Getting to Yes Workbook (New York: Penguin Books, 1995); Roger Fisher and Daniel Shapiro, *Beyond Reason: Using Emotions as You Negotiate* (New York: Penguin Books, 2006); William Ury, *Getting Past No: Negotiating in Difficult Situations*, rev. ed. (New York: Bantam Books, 1993). For discussion of interest-based negotiation concepts in a workplace context, refer to: Daniel B. Griffith and Cliff Goodwin, *Conflict Survival Kit: Tools for Resolving Conflict at Work* (Upper Saddle River, NJ: Pearson Education, Inc., 2016). These interest-based negotiation concepts are discussed throughout chapters 7 and 8.
16. Bernard S. Mayer, *Beyond Neutrality: Confronting the Crisis in Conflict Resolution* (San Francisco: Jossey-Bass, 2004).
17. Ibid., 184.

Acknowledgments

Everyday Mediator is the third book I have published, but it's my first self-published book for which I am sole author. But to suggest this was a solo effort would be an injustice to the many people who made publication possible. It's been a long bus ride, and I'm forever grateful.

Early in my journey, I found no better cheerleaders than Bridget Working, Sissy Meredith, and Charles Behling. Each in their own way remained accessible, supportive, patient, curious, and nonjudgmental over the many years it took to write (and more often not write) this book. I could always count on them for coffee or an online chat to keep me honest and not let me give up during the many times I wanted to. I am also thankful for Dimples Smith, whose spirit, inspiration, and steadfast belief in the possibilities of the everyday mediator helped me (and, I hope, readers) see the model of everyday mediation as not only life-changing but world-changing.

These friends also contributed by reviewing and offering suggestions for the book in its early stages, along with Bernie Mayer, Michael Chennault, Victoria Land, and Nan Stager. I am also grateful to the individuals who provided endorsements, many of whom offered insights on the book's content, ideas for pursuing publication, or forums in which to workshop the book's message and concepts. My thanks also to Jonathan Walker for his coaching in the later stages and helping me overcome doubt and get on with finding a route to publication.

That route led to Pithy Wordsmithery. I greatly appreciate Amelia Forczak and her vast team of professionals who managed all the details and creative work involved with publication and marketing—and managed me and my worries in the process. This includes, but is by no means limited to Deanna Novak and Karen Rowe for their editorial and project-management expertise.

Though many helped publish this book, many more helped me over the many years to develop the model of everyday mediation that I present in the book. Too numerous to name, many leaders, educators, mediators, and others afforded me opportunities to teach, train, and consult on these matters. And I am forever grateful for the thousands of learners for whom I was privileged to provide mediation and conflict-resolution training. They feed my passion for everyday mediation and reinforce in heartening and often surprising ways how the basic lessons of the everyday mediator resonate with them and positively impact their work, lives, and those they serve.

Lastly, I am grateful to my parents, Ron and Marge, who live on in my memory and made all that I've accomplished possible through their love and nurturing, and to my wife, Mary, who not only shares the bumpy ride with me but often takes the worst seat and patiently endures. It is especially her love and sacrifices that have made this book, and all my efforts behind it, possible—and worth it.

About the Author

Daniel Griffith's refreshing approach to everyday mediation grew from an abiding passion to make service as a mediator accessible to anyone. Through his training, presentations, and writing, he empowers others to rely on their innate abilities to address the everyday conflicts in the world around them. Many organizations have utilized his training to support cohorts of professionals as part of their commitment to fostering an inclusive, equitable, and welcoming work and learning culture.

Griffith is a mediator, educator, lawyer, HR leader, and writer with more than 30 years of experience working with organizations and professionals in education, nonprofit, government, and business, and for professional associations. He specializes in mediating workplace, interpersonal, management, and higher-education disputes and training lawyers, HR practitioners, managers, and other professionals in mediation, negotiation, communication, and dialogue facilitation.

Griffith teaches graduate and undergraduate courses in mediation, negotiations, and alternative dispute resolution for the Indiana University Robert H. McKinney School of Law and the Indiana University Paul H. O'Neill School of Public and Environmental Affairs. He further shares his expertise through articles, blogs, and podcasts and as a frequent contributor for HigherEdJobs.com, an online job and recruitment source. He is co-author of *The Conflict Survival*

Kit: Tools for Resolving Conflict at Work (2nd ed.) and *The Supervisor's Survival Kit* (11th ed.).

A graduate of DePauw University and the IU McKinney School of Law, Griffith holds certifications from the Society for Human Resource Management (SHRM) and the HR Certification Institute (HRCI). He is a member and currently vice president of the Indiana Association of Mediators.

www.ingramcontent.com/pod-product-compliance
Lightning Source LLC
Chambersburg PA
CBHW020535030426
42337CB00013B/854